MISSIONS STRATEGIES

of

KOREAN PRESBYTERIAN MISSIONARIES

in

CENTRAL AND SOUTHERN PHILIPPINES

REV. HAM SUK-HYUN STUDIES IN ASIAN CHRISTIANITY

Series Editor: Heerak Christian Kim (Jesus College, Cambridge)

Number 1:

MISSIONS STRATEGIES OF KOREAN PRESBYTERIAN
MISSIONARIES IN CENTRAL AND SOUTHERN PHILIPPINES
In Light of Paul's Missions Strategies
(Hoo-Soo Jose Nam)

MISSIONS STRATEGIES OF KOREAN PRESBYTERIAN MISSIONARIES IN CENTRAL AND SOUTHERN PHILIPPINES

In Light of Paul's Missions Strategies

Hoo-Soo Jose Nam

The Hermit Kingdom Press
Cheltenham ♦ Seoul ♦ Bangalore ♦ Cebu

MISSIONS STRATEGIES OF KOREAN PRESBYTERIAN MISSIONARIES IN CENTRAL AND SOUTHERN PHILIPPINES: IN LIGHT OF PAUL'S MISSIONS STRATEGIES

Copyright © 2006 by Hoo-Soo Jose Nam

All rights reserved.
No part of this work may be reproduced or transmitted in any form or by any means, electronic or mechanical, including photocopying and recording, or by any information storage (INCLUDING COMPUTER AND WEB) or retrieval system without permission from the publisher.

For information address:

The Hermit Kingdom Press
12325 Imperial Highway, Suite 156
Norwalk, California 90650
United States of America

www.TheHermitKingdomPress.com

Hermit Kingdom
12 South Bridge, Suite 370
Edinburgh, EH1 1DD
Scotland

ISBN: 0-972-38645-9 (Hardcover)
ISBN: 1-59689-060-6 (Paperback)

Library of Congress Cataloging-in-Publication Data

Nam, Hoo-Soo Jose.
  Missions strategies of Korean Presbyterian missionaries in central and southern Philippines : in light of Paul's missions strategies / Hoo-Soo Jose Nam.
    p. cm. -- (Rev. Ham Suk-Hyun studies in Asian Christianity ; 1)
  ISBN 0-9723864-5-9 (hardcover : alk. paper) -- ISBN 1-59689-060-6 (pbk. : alk. paper)
  1. Presbyterian Church--Missions--Philippines. 2. Missionaries--Korea. 3. Missions--Theory. 4. Paul, the Apostle, Saint. 5. Missions--Biblical teaching. I. Title. II. Series.
  BV3380.N36 2006
  266'.509599--dc22
                    2006017074

For My Lovely Wife, Sung-Hee

ACKNOWLEDGMENTS

This book represents my Doctor of Theology (Th.D.) dissertation submitted to Asia Baptist Graduate Theological Seminary in the Philippines in February, 2002.

The three years and four months I have spent in my "doctoral pilgrimage" involved special persons to whom I am grateful. Special appreciation goes to my wife, Sung-Hee (Eunice) Lee Nam, whose love, encouragement, understanding, patient support, and partnership in ministry sustained me in completing my doctoral studies. I am thankful to my son, Hwa-Peong (Timothy) and my daughter, Hae-Sun (Keren), for acting responsibly at home during my absence as a doctoral student. Their constant communications kept me abreast of what was going on at home and in the ministry. I would like to deeply thank my beloved parents, Suk-Lin Nam (father), and Young-Hee Kim (mother), and dear mother-in-law, Dae-Im Yoon, for their prayers and love. Special gratitude goes to my brothers, sisters, and my in-laws for showing enormous concern, love, and support during my doctoral days. I also appreciate the faithful support and unceasing prayers of my supporting churches in Korea.

A heartfelt gratitude is due to Dr. Tereso Casiño, my supervising professor, and to Dr. Edgar Auñgon, my doctoral teaching program supervisor, for their guidance and able mentorship. Deep appreciation also goes to my external reader in Korea, Dr. Hwal-Young (Gerardo) Kim, and to all professors of the Asia Baptist Graduate Theological Seminary for their insights and counsel. Special acknowledgment goes to all the Korean Presbyterian missionaries in the Visayas Presbytery, who participated in the field survey.

I appreciate the encouragement and support of my fellow Faculty members at Cebu Bible College, along with the prayers of my lovely students.

PRAISE THE LORD FOR LEADING THE WAY!
EBENEZER!

CONTENTS

ACKNOWLEDGMENT..vii

LIST OF TABLES...x

INTRODUCTION...1

CHAPTER 1: PAUL'S MISSIONS STRATEGIES IN ACTS 13-28....................11

CHAPTER 2: MISSIONS STRATEGIES OF THE KOREAN PRESBYTERIAN MISSIONARIES IN CENTRAL AND SOUTHERN PHILIPPINES..................47

CHAPTER 3: AN ANALYSIS OF THE MISSIONS STRATEGIES OF THE KOREAN PRESBYTERIAN MISSIONARIES IN CENTRAL AND SOUTHERN PHILIPPINES IN THE LIGHT OF PAUL'S MISSION'S STRATEGIES.............97

CONCLUSION..116

APPENDICES

   A. LETTER TO THE CHAIRPERSON OF A MISSIONS GROUP...121

   B. LETTER TO KOREAN PRESBYTERIAN MISSIONARIES
      IN CENTRAL AND SOUTHERN PHILIPPINES......................122

   C. MISSION STATIONS OF THE KOREAN PRESBYTERIAN
      MISSIONARIES IN CENTRAL AND SOUTHERN
      PHILIPPINES..123

   D. A SURVEY QUESTIONNAIRE FOR THE KOREAN
      PRESBYTERIAN MISSIONARIES IN CENTRAL
      AND SOUTHERN PHILIPPINES..124

WORKS CITED..132

PHOTOS...147

ABSTRACT..167

List of Tables

Table	Page
1. Ministerial Status of the Missionaries	55
2. Age Range of the Missionaries	56
3. Length of Period in Missions Work	56
4. Analysis of Ministries	57
5. Analysis of Church Growth	59
6. Effective Strategies for Early Stages of Church Planting	60
7. Strategic Place for Church Planting	61
8. Target Group of People	62
9. Primary Concern in Choosing Area for Church Planting	64
10. Type of Message	65
11. Attitude toward Other Religion	66
12. Mode of Conclusion of Preaching	67
13. Appropriate Leadership Training Program	68
14. The Period of Hold Leadership	70
15. Qualification of Being a Pastor	71
16. Women Leadership	73
17. Ideal Length of Missionary Service	74
18. Principles for a New Missionary to Follow	75

19. Gifts for Missionaries..76

20. Effectiveness of Direct Financial Support Program....................77

21. The Effectiveness of "Self-support" Principle..........................78

22. Types of Missionary in Financial Support...............................79

23. Use of Missions Funds...80

24. The Appropriate Length of Financial Support..........................82

25. Effectiveness of Cooperation...83

26. Helpfulness of Short-term Missionary....................................84

27. Level of Cooperation..85

28. Authority to Make Decision..86

29. Understanding and Participating of Support Churches................87

30. Languages Employed for Ministry..88

31. Degree of Emphasizing "Korean style"..................................89

32. Frequency to Observe "Thanksgiving Sunday"........................90

33. Special Occasions Observed..92

34. Activities Implemented in the Church...................................93

35. Frequency of Using Filipino Literary Forms............................95

36. Strengths of Missions Strategies..98

37. Weaknesses of Missions Strategies......................................106

MISSIONS STRATEGIES

of

KOREAN PRESBYTERIAN MISSIONARIES

in

CENTRAL AND SOUTHERN PHILIPPINES

Introduction

World missions is Christians' responsibility to fulfill the Great Commission of Jesus Christ (Matt. 28:19-20). To achieve the goal of world missions, missionaries are expected to set up appropriate and relevant missions strategies according to its context.

Paul's missions strategies in Acts 13-28 are fundamental principles that missionaries may employ for setting up their own missions strategies. This section sets forth three basic areas: the research problem and its setting, the importance of the study, and the research methodology.

The Research Problem and Its Setting

The research problem and its setting include the statement of the problem, sub-problems, limits of the problem, definition of terms, and basic assumptions.

The Statement of the Problem

This research proposes to study the following problem: What are the missions strategies of the Korean Presbyterian missionaries in central and southern Philippines from 1990 to 2000 which can be analyzed in the light of Paul's missions strategies?

Sub-problems

The first sub-problem is as follows: What are Paul's missions strategies evident in Acts 13-28?

The second sub-problem is as follows: What are the missions strategies of the Korean Presbyterian missionaries in central and southern Philippines from 1990 to 2000?

The third sub-problem is as follows: What are the strengths and weaknesses of missions strategies of the Korean Presbyterian missionaries in central and southern Philippines in the light of Paul's missions strategies?

Limits of the Problem

This research sought to identify the relationship between the missions strategies of the Korean Presbyterian missionaries in central and southern Philippines and the missions strategies of Paul. The study focused on missions strategies of the Korean Presbyterian missionaries in central and southern Philippines from 1990 to 2000. The research dealt only with Paul's missions strategies that can be identified in Acts 13-28.

Definition of Terms

"Mission" refers to the total works of God on behalf of the salvation of mankind. It is a comprehensive term including the upward, inward and outward ministries of the church.[1]

"Missions" is a specialized term. It refers to every attempt, effort, and practical implementation of God's mission on earth using all available methods according to each context.[2]

"A missionary" is a Christian messenger of the gospel called to carry out missions, sent forth by the authority of the Lord and the church to cross ethnic borders and cultural and religious lines.

"Strategies" are methods and plans to achieve effectively the ends of missionary purposes which have been relevantly determined by a particular group of missionaries according to each context.[3]

"Korean Presbyterian missionaries" refer to the Korean missionaries who were dispatched by different denominations which use "Korean Presbyterian Church" as their denominational name in Korea, but are working together with the Presbyterian

---

[1] George W. Peters, *A Biblical Theology of Mission* (Chicago: Moody Press, 1980), 11.

[2] Gailyn Van Rheenen, *Missions: Biblical Foundation and Contemporary Strategies* (Grand Rapids, MI: Zondervan Publishing House, 1996), 20. Lesslie Newbigin, one of the leaders of the ecumenical movement, does not distinguish "mission" and "missions." He, however, has defined missions as "particular enterprises within the total mission which have the primary intention of bringing into existence a Christian presence in a milieu where previously there was no such presence or where such presence was ineffective." Newbigin emphasized the word "intention." He notes that although many incidents in early church such as the death of Stephen, the Jerusalem church was attacked and dispersed, the scattering of believers produced and enormous missionary expansion, there was no missionary intension. But when the Antioch church, moved by the Holy Spirit, laid hands on Saul and Barnabas and "sent them off" to the Gentiles, the missionary "intension" was central. ("Cross-currents in Ecumenical and Evangelical Understandings of Mission" *International Bulletin of Missionary Research* 6 [October 1982]: 149.)

[3] C. Peter Wagner, *Frontiers in Missionary Strategy* (Chicago: Moody Press, 1978), 16.

Church of the Philippines.[4]

"Central and southern Philippines" refer to the geographical areas of the Philippines known as Visayas and Mindanao respectively.

Basic Assumptions

This research had three basic assumptions. The first basic assumption was as follows: Paul employed missions strategies which can be ascertained by examining Acts 13-28.

The second basic assumption was as follows: There are missions strategies among the Korean Presbyterian missionaries in central and southern Philippines from 1990 to 2000, and these can be identified.

The third basic assumption was as follows: There are verifiable strengths and weaknesses in the missions strategies employed by the Korean Presbyterian missionaries in central and southern Philippines, in relation to Paul's missions strategies and to the statistical growth of the church for which the Korean Presbyterian missionaries work.

The Importance of the Study

In obedience to the missions mandate of God, the Korean Presbyterian Church sent her first missionary, one of the first seven Korean Presbyterian ordained ministers, to Che-ju island which is far from mainland, but within Korean territory in 1907. Five years later, in commemoration of the organizing of the General Assembly of the Korean Presbyterian Church in 1912, the Korean Presbyterian Church dispatched her first three foreign missionaries to China.[5]

The first Korean Presbyterian missionary sent to the Philippines was Hwal-Young Kim. After Kim and his family arrived in the Philippines in March 1977, the number of Korean Presbyterian missionaries increased annually.[6] At the time of this research,

---

[4]The missionaries came from four major denominations of the Korean Presbyterian Church and their names are as follows: KPCK (Ko-sin), KPCH (Hap-dong), KPCT (Tong-hap), and KPCKH (Kai-hyuk). The Presbyterian Church of the Philippines (PCP) is a denomination that was organized by mainly KPCH missionaries in 1987, is a member church of the Philippine Council of Evangelical Church (PCEC), and is duly registered with the Security and Exchange Commission of the Philippine government. KPCK, KPCH, KPCT, KPCKH, and PCP will be used hereafter.

[5]Kyung Bae Min, *Church History of Korea* (Seoul: The Christian Literature Society, 1973), 222, 410. The first Korean missionary was Rev. Ki-Poong Lee.

[6]Hwal-Young Kim, "From Asia to Asia: A History of Cross-Cultural Missionary Work of the

there were 121 Korean missionaries who were working with the PCP in the Philippines.[7]

The first Korean Presbyterian missionary to central Philippines came to Cebu City on September 4, 1987 and started the first English worship for Filipino Presbyterian congregation on the first Sunday of January 1989.[8] With the changing of Korean government policy for traveling abroad in 1988, the number of Korean missionaries increased rapidly. As of this research thirty-one Korean Presbyterian missionaries (Fourteen married male, fourteen married female, and three single women) were working with PCP in central and southern Philippines.[9]

Alongside with the growth of the missions movement and an increasing number of missionaries in central and southern Philippines, Korean Presbyterian missionaries have encountered many problems in their ministries. First, the central and southern regions of the Philippines are geographically too immense to cover with a limited number of missionaries. Over 6,000 out of 7,107 islands are scattered in this region and the inhabitants of each island use a different language or dialect.[10] These situations cause enormous communication and transportation problems to missionaries.

Second, learning languages is one of the greatest barriers for Korean missionaries. Since the structure and sound of the Korean language are much different from that of English, Korean missionaries find themselves learning English first when assigned to the Philippines. After English, Korean missionaries have to struggle with another language, the target area language, for example, Cebuano, Hiligaynon, Boholanon, Tagalog, specific Muslim languages or others.[11]

Presbyterian Church in Korea (Hap-dong), 1959-1992" (D.Miss. Diss., Reformed Theological Seminary, 1993), 191.

[7]Tae-Yun Hwang, ed., *Directory of Korean Missions and Missionaries in the Philippines* "1999" (Manila: The Association of Korean Missions in the Philippines, 1999), 93-376. The researcher counted manually the number of missionaries who work with PCP.

[8]The researcher was the first Korean Presbyterian missionary to the central Philippines. Right after he arrived in Cebu City, he organized a Korean congregation and started Korean worship on the last Sunday of September 1987. While he took language training (English and Cebuano), he and the Korean congregation invited several Filipino friends to their worship services. During the first several months with Filipinos, he led the worship in Korean with written English translation. When the number of the Filipino attendance increased, the church felt the need to divide the group into two: Korean worship in the morning and English worship in the afternoon. This change took place on the first Sunday of January 1989. However, as the number of both Korean and Filipino congregation bigger and their activities increased, the Korean congregation moved to another place for a new meeting place. All furniture and decorations were turned over to the Filipino congregation to use in July 1990.

[9]*Directory of Churches and Pastors of Visayas Presbytery* (Cebu, Philippines: Visayas Presbytery, 1999), n.p.

[10]Conrado M. Lancion, Jr., *Fast Facts About Philippine Provinces* (Manila: Tahanan Books, 1995), 9.

[11]Cebuano, one out of 168 languages in the Philippines, is a major language in central and southern

Third, the mosaic of people in the Philippines bewilders Korean missionaries. Since Korea is a mono-race, mono-language, and monoculture country, Korean missionaries experience confusion when they encounter various races, languages, and cultures within a country. Thus, they are puzzled about how to interact with different people in different ways at the same time.

Fourth, added to the problems mentioned above, the dominant religions in central and southern Philippines which Korean missionaries are not familiar with make life more difficult in the field. The major forces of Roman Catholicism, Islam, and New People's Army have built their fortresses in this region. Facing these problems requires relevant, effective, and biblical missions strategies.

On the other hand, the more serious problem Korean missionaries face is their attitude toward and limited knowledge of missions strategies. Often they seem to lack the awareness about what the Bible teaches concerning missions strategies or of the lessons learned in the history of missions work. Some Korean missionaries attempted to plant Korean-style church and stressed Korean-style church management. This caused problems between the missionary and Filipino congregations, and even among missionaries themselves.

The researcher has worked with Korean Presbyterian missionaries in central and southern Philippines for more than twelve years, and has seen many of them struggling as they approach the problems mentioned above. The greatest problem of Korean Presbyterian missionaries in central and southern Philippines today seems to arise from the use of culturally irrelevant and ineffective missions strategies. This serious and undesirable situation, thus accounts for the importance of this study in order to seek relevant and effective missions strategies the Korean Presbyterian missionaries in central and southern Philippines may adapt.

Paul stands out as a pioneer in cross-cultural missions in the New Testament. "Paul had the mind of scholar," observes J. Herbert Kane, "the heart of an evangelist, the discipline of a soldier, the devotion of a lover, the vision of a seer, the zeal of a reformer, and the passion of a prophet."[12] Roland Allen observes that some scholars try to stain Paul's ministries by insisting that he "was an exceptional man living in exceptional times, preaching under exceptional circumstances; that he enjoyed advantages in his birth, his education, his call, his mission, his relationship to his hearers, such as have been enjoyed by no other; and that he enjoyed advantages in the peculiar constitution of society at the moment of his call such as to render his work

---

Philippines. Over fifteen million people use Cebuano as their mother tongue today. However, Filipino and English are government official languages. English is the medium of education (Patrick Johnstone, *Operation World*, 5th ed. [Carlisle, UK: OM Publishing, 1993: reprint, with corrections, Carlisle, UK: OM Publishing, 1995], 448).

[12] J. Herbert Kane, *Christian Missions in Biblical Perspective* (Grand Rapids, MI: Baker Book House, 1976), 72.

quite exceptional."[13]   Allen, however, defended these accusation against Paul as follows: (1) Paul's method was to follow the guidance of the Holy Spirit, not the advantages of exceptional circumstances (2) modern missionaries have more advantages than Paul: Paul had only Old Testament but modern missionaries have the whole Bible plus printing press, and (3) Paul was endowed with exceptional genius and his works were endowed with a universal character.[14]

The social, cultural, political, and religious circumstances of Paul's age are different from those of today. These differences, however, do not negate the reliability of the Bible. As a source of missionary methodology, the principles of Paul's missions strategies obviously continue to enlighten contemporary missionaries.[15]

The primary purpose of this research, therefore, was to analyze the strengths and weaknesses of the missions strategies of the Korean Presbyterian missionaries in central and southern Philippines in the light of Paul's missions strategies. This dissertation sought to discover similarities and differences between Paul's missions strategies and those of the Korean Presbyterian missionaries in central and southern Philippines. It attempted to project the missions strategies of the Korean Presbyterian missionaries in central and southern Philippines into Paul's missions strategies so that the former may reflect on their missions strategies and employ effective, relevant, and biblically-oriented missions strategies.

Research Methodology

This paper used both literary and field survey research methods. Literary research was employed mainly for chapter one and parts of chapter two and three, while survey research was conducted in chapter two.

Literary Research

Chapter one utilized literary research to investigate Paul's missions strategies as a criterion for analyzing the current missions strategies being practiced among the

---

[13]Roland Allen, *Missionary Methods: St Paul's or Ours?* (Grand Rapids, MI: Wm. B. Eerdmans Publishing Co., 1979), 4.

[14]Ibid.

[15]Edward C. Pentecost, *Issues in Missiology: An Introduction* (Grand Rapids, MI: Baker Book House, 1982), 65-77. David J. Hesselgrave also supports that Pauline strategy is applicable today (*Planting Churches Cross-Culturally: A Guide For Home and Foreign Missions* [Grand Rapids, MI: Baker Book House, 1991], 55).

Korean Presbyterian missionaries in central and southern Philippines. The primary focus of the study was based on the book of Acts chapters 13-28. The criterion for choosing this part of the Bible was that Acts 13-28 exposes the fundamental principles of Paul's missions strategies; e. g., the principle of planting churches, preaching the gospel, equipping leaders, financing ministry, team ministry, and contextualized communication.[16] Books, articles, and other mission-related materials were consulted to understand Paul's missions strategies as understood from different perspectives. A part of chapter two and chapter three also used literary research.

Chapter three integrated the materials of the first two chapters. It sought to compare Paul's missions strategies and the missions strategies that have been practiced for a decade by the Korean Presbyterian missionaries in central and southern Philippines. As the objective criteria for judging the strengths and weaknesses of the missions strategies, available works such as the number of churches, ministries planted by missionaries, the number of their national co-workers, and the number of baptized members of their church were employed.

The venues of the research were the libraries of the following institutions: Philippine Baptist Theological Seminary, Baguio City; Asia Pacific Theological Seminary, Baguio City; Presbyterian Theological Seminary, Dasmarinas City, Cavite; Cebu Bible College, Mandaue City, Philippines; Korea Theological Seminary, Chunan; Kosin Universiy, Pusan, Korea.

Survey Research

Chapter two utilized the survey research to discover the missions strategies of the Korean Presbyterian missionaries in central and southern Philippines. There were two areas of the survey research: archival records and self-administered questionnaire.

<u>Historical Records Survey</u>

The researcher studied available official and personal records of and materials on missions activities of the four missions groups and individual missionaries in central and southern Philippines working with the PCP in relation to their current missions strategies. The main source of the study were the available minutes of meetings of the four missions groups, brief history made by missions group, the records of the General Assembly of the PCP, and the journals of the Visayas Presbytery.[17] This research utilized other materials such as newsletters, prayer requests, personal letters, e-mail letters, personal face to face and telephone interview, and other available related

---

[16]These six items will outline the fundamental principles of Paul's missions strategies in Chapter 1.

[17]Presbytery is the second highest and regional jurisdictional meeting of the Presbyterian Church government system. The highest national body is the General Assembly.

materials.

Self-administered Questionnaire

A letter to the chairpersons of the four missions groups requesting them to endorse the sending of questionnaires to the missionaries of each group in central and southern Philippines and gathering information were sent through electronic mail (e-mail) system.[18] The researcher contacted those chairpersons personally face to face and through telephone. This letter introduced the researcher and explained the purpose of the research project.

A letter accompanied with the questionnaire to the respondents introduced the researcher, explained the value and purpose of the research project, and provided instructions on the procedure and conduct of the questionnaire.[19] The researcher visited Davao city once to distribute the questionnaire directly to the respondents. Respondents who resided in Cebu city and its vicinity received the questionnaire directly from the researcher. The researcher used the e-mail system for sending the questionnaire to respondents who live outside Cebu city and used telephone calls to make follow up. The questionnaire written in both Korean and English for the missionaries used to gather information that may reveal their missions strategies which they employed in the last decade.[20]

There were thirty-one Korean Presbyterian missionaries working with PCP in central and southern Philippines. The assigned areas and number of missionaries were as follows: twelve missionaries in Cebu City and its vicinity, four missionaries in Iloilo City, four missionaries in Dumaguete City, and eleven missionaries in Davao City and its vicinity.[21] These thirty-one missionaries comprised the population of the survey and all of them returned the questionnaire to the researcher by hand, through e-mail and other mailing system. The collected questionnaires were scored, analyzed, and the response percentages computed. In the light of the survey data, interpretation is presented in Chapter two.

Treatment of Data

The researcher tallied and tabulated the data gathered from primary sources such as newsletters, prayer requests, souvenir program, personal interview, personal letter, and journals of Visayas Presbytery and General Assembly of the PCP meetings. The

---

[18]See Appendix A.

[19]See Appendix B.

[20]See Appendix D.

[21]See Appendix C. A missionary wife was counted as an individual missionary.

data provided by respondents were analyzed by employing some statistical tools. These data were needed to ensure the credibility of the analysis.[22] The data gathered for this study were computed in percentages and ranks. Computed value was up to the second digit. The researcher employed tables to convey the analysis in a clear fashion.

Statistical tools utilized in this study was mainly "mean." The "mean" was used to measure regular distribution of the topics of interest through ranking. The formula for the "mean" was as follows: $\bar{x} = X/N$. Where "$\bar{x}$" is the "mean" for the arithmetic average observations. "X" is the frequency or each individual observation. "N" is the total number of observations or the number of score.[23]

The rank responses were given arbitrary weight mean (or weighted value) stress corresponding to the ranks indicated. In case of that there was five items in one question, the first in rank was given a weighted mean of five points; the second in rank was given four points; the third in rank was given three points; the fourth in rank was given two points, and the fifth in rank was given one point value. The arbitrary point values are based upon the importance of the rank criteria per item asked in the questionnaire. The responses were tallied by ranks, then, multiplied by their respective weighted point added and divided by the total number of responses. The formula used for the average weighted mean for the solution of each item is as follows: $WM = \Sigma (F)(W) / \Sigma F$. Where "WM" is equal to weighted mean, "F" is equal to number of tallied responses per rank criteria, "W" is equal to arbitrary point value per rank, and ΣF is equal to total number of respondents for all ranks in the item.

The weighted mean were interpreted and classified by the range interval formula, namely, the ratio of the difference between the highest and lowest possible score by the number of steps needed. The range interval was computed as follows: 5-1/five = four/five = 0.8. The range values were distributed equally for the rank interpretation as follows:

Weighted Mean Scaled	Rank Criteria
4.3 to 5.0	First in Rank
3.5 to 4.2	Second in Rank
2.7 to 3.4	Third in Rank
1.9 to 2.6	Fourth in Rank
1.0 to 1.8	Fifth in Rank

---

[22] Anselmo Lupdag, *Educational Psychology* (Quezon City, Philippines: National Book Store, Inc., 1984), 26. Lupdag notes, "Statistics aims to organize a large amount of data so that it would somehow make sense" (Ibid.).

[23] Arlene Fink, *How to Analyze Survey Data* (Thousand Oaks, CA: SAGE Publishing, 1995), 17.

These weighted mean criteria were utilized throughout the entire analysis of the responses. The other items were analyzed by the number of responses per item.

Chapter One

PAUL'S MISSIONS STRATEGIES IN ACTS 13-28

Paul is considered as the first full-scale cross-cultural missionary whose ministry extends beyond the geographical and cultural boundary of Judea. Paul, thus, overcomes the limited salvation concept of Judaism to reach the Gentiles theologically. Paul's missions strategies that made his activities possible are revealed in Acts 13-28.[24]

This chapter explores Paul's missions strategies which are the foundations of his successful ministries as follows: (1) strategies in planting church; (2) strategies in preaching the gospel; (3) strategies in equipping leaders; (4) strategies in financing the ministry; (5) strategies in team ministry; and (6) strategies in contextualized communication. These six missions strategies are selected as endorsed by missions and Bible scholars and their relevance to the Korean Presbyterian missionaries in central and southern Philippines.[25] Missions strategies include methods and plans to achieve

---

[24]Donald McGavran asserts that while Paul was in Antioch, he devised a strategy for reaching a great part of the Mediterranean world with the gospel (The Bridges of God [New York: Friendship Press, 1955], 25-35). Herbert Kane notes that Paul has little or no strategy if by strategy is meant a deliberate, well-formulated, duly executed plan of action based on human observation and experience (Christian Missions in Biblical Perspective [Grand Rapids, MI: Baker Book House, 1976], 73).

[25]Many scholars (e.g., Roland Allen, Ho-Jin Chun, J. Herbert Kane, Melvin Hodges, David J. Hesselgrave, David J. Bosch, Wayne Allen, David Schmidt, among others) count these as major missions strategies of Paul, though not all of them refer to all the six topics in the same time and order. Herbert Kane finds nine strategies as follows: (1) Paul maintaines close contact with the home base, (2) Paul confines his efforts to his efforts to four provinces, (3) Paul concentrates on the large cities, (4) Paul makes the synagogue the scene of his chief labors, (5) Paul prefers to preach to responsive peoples, (6) Paul baptizes converts on confession of their faith, (7) Paul remains long enough in one place to establish, (8) Paul make ample use of fellow workers, and (9) Paul becomes all things to all men (*Christian Missions in Biblical Perspective*, 73-85).

effectively the ends of missions purposes, determined relevantly by a particular group of missionaries according to each context. This chapter argues that when a missionary is aware of these biblical missions strategies prior to his or her ministries, the missionary may reduce mistakes and consequently achieves a better result. Paul's six missions strategies will be examined respectively.

Paul's Strategies in Planting Church

Paul devotes himself to plant churches and is a master builder of the church.[26] Although Paul's period of missionary work spans only a little more than ten years, yet, he plants healthy and growing churches in four provinces of the Roman Empire, namely, Galatia, Macedonia, Achaia and Asia. This section explores Paul's strategies in planting church as follows: (1) choosing strategic location; (2) selecting receptive people; and (3) employing effective methods.

Choosing Strategic Location

Paul chooses urban areas rather than remote villages to plant churches in his entire missionary career. This section shows the demography of Paul's target cities, factors to choose cities, and the worldwide vision beyond the cities based on Acts 13-28.

The Demography of Cities During Paul's Time

Paul prefers larger cities to plant a church like the cases in Antioch, Philippi, Thessalonica, Corinth, and Rome not because of their convenience, but because of their strategic importance.[27] In his missionary journey, Paul moves to major cities, looks for

---

[26]Ben Sawatsky emphasizes that planting church is to enter the mainstream of God's plan for the missionary enterprise ("What It Takes to be a Church Planter," *Evangelical Missions Quarterly* 27 [Oct. 1991]: 342). C. Peter Wagner also supports church planting by contending that the single most effective evangelistic methodology under heaven is planting new churches. He enumerates five reasons of which church planting is at the central position in planning strategies for church ministry and mission as follows: (1) Church planting is biblical, (2) Church planting means denominational survival, (3) Church planting develops new leadership, (4) Church planting stimulates existing churches, and (5) Church planting is efficient (*Church Planting for a Greater Harvest* [Ventura, CA: Regal Books, 1990], 11, 19-21).

[27]Michael Green points Paul's strategy of urban concentration as follows: "The acts of the Apostles records his visit to city after city of importance: Antioch, the third city in the Empire, Philippi; the Roman *colonia;* Thessalonica, the principal metropolis of Macedonia; Corinth, the capital of Greece under Roman administration; Paphos, the center of Roman rule in Cyprus; Ephesus, the principal city of the province of Asia. It is hard to escape the conclusion that this succession of important cities, which Paul made the centers, sometimes of, prolonged missionary activity, was not hit on by accident. It was part of a definite plan for planting the good news in key positions throughout the Empire" (*Evangelism in the Early Church* [Grand Rapids, MI: William B. Eerdmans Publishing Company, 1970], 262). See also J. L. Blevins, "Acts

a Jewish synagogue, and proclaims Jesus to the Jews and the Gentile God-fearers on every Sabbath (13:5, 14; 14:1; 17:1-2, 10, 17; 18:4, 19, 26).[28] Paul's cities are the main centers as far as communication, culture, commerce, politics, and religion are concerned (16:12; 19:10, 27, 38-41; 1Thes. 1:8). In Paphos, Paul evangelizes the proconsul, Sergius Paulus (13:6-12). Philippi is a Roman colony and the leading biggest city of Macedonia (16:12). Athens is a city of the most prominent political, cultural, academic, religious, social, and amphitheatric center in Roman Empire (18:16-21). Ephesus is a commercial, cultural, sports, and religious center in Asia minor(19:27-41). There are well constructed stone paved Roman military roads that connect city to city. In brief, all the cities or towns in which Paul's church planting activities take place are centers of Roman administrations, of Greek civilization, of Jewish influence, of Roman military camp, and of some commercial importance.[29]

Factors in Choosing Cities

Paul seems to have two reasons to choose cities. The major cities which Paul normally visits have the representative nature for the surrounding area and have a Jewish synagogue that bridges the gospel with the Gentiles.

The Representative Nature of Cities

Paul would choose cities because of the representative nature of the cities. All cities in which Paul lays the foundations for a Christian community are strategic centers, from which the gospel has advanced to all provincial villages, surrounding towns, and countryside, accompanied with the merchandisers, Roman military personnel, and other travelers (19:10).[30]

The Accessibility through Synagogue

In most major cities of Roman Empire in Paul's time, there are Jewish synagogues and Paul takes the advantages of utilizing these synagogues as a stepping stone for

---

13-19: The Tale of Three Cities," *Review and Expositor* 87 (March 1990): 439-50.

[28]Edward R. Dayton and David A. Fraser, "Strategy," in *Perspectives on the World Christian Movement*, ed. Ralph D. Winter and Steven C. Hawthorne (Pasadena, CA: William Carey Library, 1981), 569.

[29]Roland Allen, *Missionary Methods: St. Paul's or Ours?* (Grand Rapids, MI: Wm. B. Eerdmans Publishing Company, 1962), 13. Merrill C. Tenney, *New Testament Survey* (Grand Rapids, MI: William B. Eerdmans Publishing Co., 1961), 20-45.

[30]F. F. Bruce, *Paul: Apostle of the Heart Set Free* (Grand Rapids, MI: William Eerdmans Publishing Company, 1978), 475. See also Donald Guthrie, *New Testament Introduction* (Downers Grove, IL: Inter-Varsity Press, 1970), 566.

evangelism (13:5, 14; 14:1; 17:1-2, 10, 17; 18:4, 19, 26). Every synagogue is a ring of Gentiles. In most synagogues, Greek God-fearers who have been drawn by the witness of the Jews to the worship of one God are ready to hear the gospel from Paul (Acts 13:43, 48; 17:4, 12; 18:4). Paul favors to preach the gospel in the synagogues due to the easy access to open-minded people (13:43; 14:1, 27; 17:2).[31] The synagogue is one of the most strategic points for Paul to reach both the Jewish Diaspora and the Gentiles.

The Worldwide Vision

Paul extends missionary activities not only to the major cities of the four provinces of Roman Empire and their vicinities, but also worldwide. Since Rome is the capital of the empire or the capital of the known world in his time, Paul contemplates a visit to the metropolis which apparently God sanctions (19:21; 23:11). Paul obviously aknowledges the importance and effect of Rome for the expansion of church to the rest of the world.[32] He seems to have a plan to preach the gospel even to the geographical end of the earth. In his letter to Romans, he mentions his wish to visit Spain, the western half of the Roman Empire and the known end of the earth in his time, with the help of the Christians in Rome (Rom. 15:24).[33]

Selecting Receptive Peoples

Paul seems to believe that every people group on earth has the right to hear the gospel and he feels the responsibility to preach the gospel to them (26:16-18). Paul, however, has to visit places where people are receptive to the gospel. Paul does not cling to people who vehemently and consistently refuse the message and persecute the messenger. Paul, thus, rather moves on to another group of people who are responsive.

Focusing on Receptive People

---

[31] R. C. H. Lenski, *The Interpretation of the Acts of the Apostles II*, trans. Yeong-Bae Cha (Seoul: Baek Hap Publishing Company, 1979), 170.

[32] Paul acknowledges the advantages of the Roman citizenship holder and he sometimes uses it when it helps advance the gospel. The Roman citizenship gives him tremendous opportunities to share the gospel (Acts 16:37; 22:25-29). See also David J. Bosch, *Transforming Mission* (Maryknoll, New York: Orbis Books, 1991), 130.

[33] Why Paul chooses Spain, as his next destination of missions trip is unclear. James Dunn presents three probable reasons as follows: (1) Spain was well regarded by Romans, attracting many businessmen and veterans. Spain would very likely have had much greater appeal than other regions, (2) There were probably Jews settlement and synagogues, and (3) Paul may understand Spain to be the Tarshish of Isa 66:19: only when he has brought Christian representatives from Spain (Rom 15:16, 24) as part of his collection enterprise (Rom 15:25-27) will the "full number of the Gentiles come in" (Rom 15:25) and the grand final of Rom 11:25-27 unfold (*Romans 9-16*, vol. 38$_B$, *Word Biblical Commentary* [Dallas, TX: Word Books Publisher, 1988], 872).

Although God calls Paul to preach the gospel for the Gentiles (22:21), the latter always feels a burden for Jews as he says, "We had to speak the Word of God to you first" (13:46). Whenever he moves to a new region, Paul makes it his strategy to preach the gospel in Jewish synagogue and meet Jews first particularly during his first and second missionary journeys (13:5; 17:2; 18:19). In the synagogue, Paul usually starts his message from the Jewish history and concludes it with Jesus Christ through whom both the Jews and the Gentiles are saved (13:16-41; 17:2-3; 18:5).[34] Every time, Paul's preaching divides the congregation into two parts: those who accept the message and follow him, and those who reject the truth and oppose him. The former receptive people are mostly the proselytes and God-fearing Gentiles (13:43; 14:1; 16:5, 15, 34; 17:4, 12, 34; 18:8; 19:19). The latter opposite people are Jews who listen most attentively as long as Paul speaks of Israel's glorious history. But the moment Paul tries to prove that Jesus of Nazareth is Israel's long-promised Messiah they turn against him and raise a riot in an attempt to destroy him.[35] Towards these hostile Jews, Paul boldly says: "We had to speak the Word of God to you first. Since you reject it and do not consider yourselves worthy of eternal life, we now turn to the Gentiles" (13:46; 18:6; 22:21; 28:28).[36]

Favoring No Specific Class of People

Although Paul prefers to plant churches among receptive peoples, he has no favored class of people to whom he gives a special attention. It appears to indicate that Paul favors a certain class of people because he always preaches in the Jewish synagogues first in a new place. But it is just an opening stage of ministry in a new region, not as a matter of favoritism. The Jews would soon expel Paul out of the synagogue. But he would continue to preach the gospel in the house of a man or woman of good repute like Lydia in Philippi, Jason in Thessalonica, or Titus Justus in Corinth (16:15; 17:7; 18:7). Paul is a great scholar who disputes with a group of Epicurean and Stoic philosophers who spend time talking about and listening to the latest ideas in Athens.[37] He, however, does not seem to seek particularly to attract the

---

[34] In a traditional synagogue, a ruler of the synagogue who is in charge of the building and all activities used to invite some suitable person to deliver an address among its regular members or visitors. Paul as a visitor rabbi used to be invited to speak a word of exhortation to the gathering (F. F. Bruce, *The Book of the Acts* [Grand Rapids, MI: Wm. B. Eerdmans Publishing Company, 1984], 267).

[35] See Acts 13:45, 50; 14:5, 19; 17:5, 13; 18:6, 12; 20:3; 21:27-32; 22:22; 23:15; 25:2; 26:28; 28:24-25.

[36] Allen has a pertinent comment on Paul's selecting receptive peoples thus:
"St. Paul did not establish himself in a place and go on preaching for years to men who refused to act on his preaching…if they rejected him, he rejected them. The 'shaking of the lap,' the 'shaking of the dust from the feet,' the refusal to teach those who refused to act on the teaching, was a vital part of the Pauline presentation of the Gospel. He did not simply 'go a way,' he openly rejected those who showed themselves unworthy of his teaching" (75).

[37] Athens was the native home of Socrates and Plato, the adopted home of Aristotle, Epicurus, and Zeno. Athens illustrates to what great heights of achievement man can ascend and still be ignorant of God.

scholars, the officials, and the philosophers (17:18, 21).

That a large number of God-fearing Greeks and not a few prominent women believe and join him does not connote that Paul prefers to evangelize this class of people more (17:4, 12). Luke describes Paul as an evangelist-missionary without regards to classes thus: "While Paul was waiting for them in Athens, he was greatly distressed to see that the city was full of idols. So he reasoned in the synagogue with the Jews and the God-fearing Greeks, as well as in the marketplace day by day with those who happened to be there"(17:16, 17). Paul prefers no specific class of people to evangelize, whether they were well educated, wealthy, or high positioned class of people.[38]

Employing Effective Methods

Paul employs relevant and appropriate methods for planting churches in his time. In this section, his house church and household evangelism methods will be discussed. Added to these will be the following methods: personal evangelism, evangelism in public place, shorter stays in one place, and role modeling in a local church.

House Churches

Athens illustrates what knowledge amounts to apart from divine revelation. Athens gave civilized man his working vocabulary in every field of knowledge such as philosophy, literature, architect, mathematic, astronomy, logic, biology, ethic, mythology, and political science. Greek civilization, however, was spiritually bankrupt. Athens created a pantheon of fallen gods. The savagery and immorality of their gods was fabled, and their theology was a mass of contradictory fables. They had no knowledge of salvation, no divine inspiration. If a Greek wanted to get drunk he turned to Dionysius; if he wanted to indulge his lust he had Aphrodite; Hermes helped him if he decided to steal. Zeus, who headed the Greek pantheon, was savage and lustful. Since the gods of Greeks had no morals, so were their worshipers. Neither purity and humanity, nor mercy found a patron among the gods. God gave human wisdom ample time to demonstrate what it could do. After the Greek world demonstrated its moral and spiritual bankruptcy and showed that human knowledge and intellectualism was not only incapable of finding God but was actually wandering further and further from God, Jesus Christ came. As a Hellenist Jew, Paul would already know much about Athens (John Phillips, *Exploring Acts: Volume Two, Acts 13-28* [Chicago, IL: Moody Press, 1986], 116-17).

[38]Allen concludes that the majority of Paul's converts were of the lower commercial and working classes, laborers, freed-men, and slavers; but that Paul himself did not deliberately aim at any class (75). Wayne A. Meeks notes that Celsus, a second century pagan author who first took Christianity seriously enough to write a book against it, alleged that the church deliberately excluded educated people because the religion was attractive only to the foolish, dishonorable and stupid, and only slaves, women, and little children. However, Meeks also cites some recent scholars like Gerd Theissen who finds leading figures in the Christian groups in Corinth who belong to a relatively high economic and social level (*The First Urban Christians* [New Heaven: Yale University Press. 1983], 51-53).

One of Paul's unique church planting methods is starting a church in a private house with the household first.[39] Lydia, a dealer in purple cloth in Philippi, invites Paul and Silas to her home and the two apostles plant a church in her house (16:14, 15). It is a typical type of house church in Acts. When the Jews in Corinth reject Paul from the Synagogue, Paul moves to the house of Titius Justus (18:7). Following Paul's move to Justus' house, it is easy to imagine that Paul starts a church in his house. To the church elders of Ephesus, he declares that he taught the gospel from house to house (20:20). No biblical evidence indicates that Paul rents a house and remits the rental or constructs a church building for any local congregation. Paul mentions various house churches that he plants during his missionary journeys in his epistles.[40] It is through the household and the house church that Christianity first puts down its roots, grows to undermine the old civic values, and reshapes the spiritual landscape of the cities.[41]

Household Conversion

In the early century of the New Testament, household conversion and household baptism are common. Luke provides ample cases of household conversion and household baptism.[42] When Lydia responds to Paul's message, Paul baptizes Lydia and her household together (16:15). To the trembling Philippian jailor, Paul says that he and his household would be saved and Paul baptizes the jailor and the whole household together (16:30-34). Crispus, the synagogue ruler in Corinth, and his household believe together (18:8). Priscilla and Aquila are a couple and would soon

---

[39]Del Birkey depicts the house church as follows: "Actually, in any important city of the first century world, if a person had asked somebody for directions to a church, he or she would have been directed to someone's home." His definition of a house church is "an indigenous and self-functioning church small enough to gather together in a

home or similar surroundings." He predicts that "if futurologists are on target, house church networks will greatly accelerate by the year 2000" ("The House Church: A Missiological Model," *Missiology* 19 [January 1991]: 69-70).

[40]The list includes (1)Priscilla and Aquila and the house church (Rom 16:3-5, 1 Cor 16:19), (2) Aristobulus and his household (Rom 16:10), (3) Narcissus and his household (Rom 16:11), (4) Rufus and his mother (Rom 16:15), (5) Gaius and the house Church (Rom 16:23), (6) Chloe's household (1 Cor 1:11), (7) Stephanas' household
(1 Cor 1:16, 16:15), (8) Caesar's household (Phil 4:22), (9) Nympha's house church (Col 4:15), (10) Onesiphorus and his household (2 Tim 1:16), (11) a certain household (Titus 1:11), and (12) Philemon's household and the house church (Phlm 2).

[41]Robin Lane Fox, *Pagans and Christianity* (New York: Alfred A. Knopf Publisher, 1989), 89. J. Gresham Machen points that the early church used to meet in private houses (The Literature and History of New Testament Times, trans. Hyo-Seong Kim [Seoul: Seong Kwang Publication, 1980], 511).

[42]Bradley Blue, "Acts and the House Church," in *The Book of Acts in Its First Century Setting*, ed. David W. J. Gill and Conrad Gempf (Grand Rapids, MI: William B. Eerdmans Publishing Company, 1994), 120.

become Paul's sincere co-workers (18:2, 18, 26). Paul, thus, takes the unity of the family seriously. In Paul's experience, when salvation is offered to the head of the household, it is a great opportunity for the rest of the family, dependents, and servants to hear and respond to the gospel (16:15, 31).[43]

Personal Evangelism

Paul uses personal conversations for evangelism (17:17). His explicit practice is to teach anything that would help people both in public and private houses (20:20). To do this, Paul would share the gospel personally with other Gentile tent makers during the weekdays, while he is engaging in making tents in the marketplace in Corinth (18:3). In Paphos, for instance, Paul shares the gospel personally to Sergius Paulus, the proconsul, an intelligent man (13:7). The jailor and his household in Philippi hear the gospel privately from Paul after midnight (16:25-28). Felix, the Roman governor to Judea, and Drusilla, Felix's Jewish wife, hear the gospel on righteousness, self-control, and judgment to come from Paul in their office (24:24-26). Like Paul's other formal speeches, the aim of his personal sharing of the gospel is to convict sin, with the call to repentance and faith. These are the facets of Paul's procedure in proclaiming the gospel (20:21).[44]

Evangelism in Public Place

Paul would debate often with Jews, other religious leaders, and philosophers in public places. He would reason with the Jews in the synagogue declaring that Jesus is the Messiah (13:45; 14:3; 15:2; 17:2, 17; 18:4, 19:8-9). Paul discusses the gospel with

---

[43] I. Howard Marshall, *The Acts of the Apostles: An Introduction and Commentary* (Grand Rapids, MI: Wm. B. Eerdmans Publishing Company, 1980), 273. Allan M. Harman argues that God makes his covenant with the head of each household and it will continue to the next generations (*Covenant and Missions* [Pusan, Korea: Kosin University Press, 1999], 10-15). Birkey traced back the origin of the house church. He concludes that "it begins from the conception of the relationship between God and mankind. The fundamental emphasis in the New Testament on the church as the family of God and the household of faith is exactly what we should expect (Rom 8:15-16; Gal 4:5-7; 6:10; Eph 2:19; 3:14-15; 5:1; 6:23). There the church is consistently a house

church, explicitly or implicitly... and provided Paul the paramount sociological model whose ramifications are seen everywhere. Furthermore, the churches that meet in their house intensified the emphasis on interpersonal family life, and reflects a Hebrew model of Christian education where parents are the primary influencers. Since household and family are universal norms in cultures everywhere, missionaries who maximize a 'family of God' household consciousness in planting church structures are most congruent with the apostolic missions ideal"(70). See also C. Kirk Hadaway, Stuart A. Wright, and Francis M. DuBose, *Home Cell Groups and House Churches*, (Nashville, TN: Broadman Press, 1987), 57. See also Ho-Jin Jun, *Missiology* (Seoul: The Korea Society of Reformed Faith and Conduct, 1989), 80.

[44] Harman, 63-66.

the people who crowed in the public market (17:17), and disputes with religious leaders and philosophers (17:22).[45] Reasoning with people is Paul's practice, so he could present the gospel, especially in his later missionary journey. The Greek imperfect verb, διελέγετο, which means 'he used to reason . . . and tried to persuade' supports the assertion that Paul's public debating is part of his habit (18:4).[46]

Shorter Stay in One Place

Paul stays in each place just long enough to establish a church. Acts depicts him as someone who does not stay long in one city. Circumstances would cut his stay short in most places because the unbelieving Jews stir up the citizens to drive him out of town.[47] Besides the persecution of the Jews and the Gentiles, there seem to be other reasons why Paul's staying in one place is short. First, since God calls him to proclaim the gospel to the Jewish Diaspora and the Gentiles, the geographical area is too vast for him to cover with limited personnel.[48] Paul, then, moves from one place to another quick than others would think. Second, Paul concentrates his efforts on the so-called "receptive people." When he meets resistant people, he leaves the place immediately and looks for another receptive region (13:51; 18:6). Third, Paul hands over his ministry quickly to the local leadership and moves to other place (14:23-26). Fourth, Paul moves from place to place to follow up people whom he evangelized. He would revisit the churches that he once planted in order to encourage the members (14:20-26; 15:36-41; 18:23).[49] Paul does not seem to remain in one place, although he continues to care for a local church after leaves the place. Soon after he appoints elders who could lead the church, Paul would leave for other regions.

<u>Role Modeling in the Church</u>

Paul strives to be a model to young believers, elders of the church, and co-

---

[45]Epicureans were influential only in the educated upper classes. They insisted the life's goal is pleasure-the lack of physical pain and emotional disturbance. Stoics were more popular, opposed pleasure, and criticized Epicureans (Craig S. Keener, *The IVP Bible Background Commentary: New Testament*, [Downers Grove, IL: InterVarsity Press, 1993], 372). See also F. F. Bruce, *New Testament History*, trans. Yong-Wha Na (Seoul: Christian Literature Crusade, 1983), 62-71.

[46]Harman, 68.

[47]See Acts 13:50; 14:5, 19; 16:39; 17:5, 13; 18:6, 12.

[48]See Acts 13:3, 4, 47; 16:10; 18:9-10; 22:23; 23:11; 26:17-18.

[49]Soon-Tae Kwon, "An Analysis of the Contemporary Models of Missions Among the Selected Baptist Churches in Seoul, Korea in the Light of Paul's Model of Missions" (Th.D. diss., Asia Baptist Graduate Theological Seminary, 2000), 27-28. See also Robert L. Maddox Jr., *Layman's Bible Book Commentary: Acts, vol. 19* (Nashville, Tennessee: Broadman Press, 1979), 78.

workers. As a model to young believers, he avoids not being idle; rather, he works hard and supplies his own needs, the needs of his companions, or weaker local churches (18:3; 20:34-35)[50]. As a model to elders, he understands how to watch over himself and all the flock of which the Holy Spirit has made him an overseer. To the elders of the church in Ephesus, Paul testifies of how he never stops warning each believer night and day with tears (20:28-32). As a model to co-workers in ministry, he humbles himself and aims to finish the race, thereby, completing the task the Lord Jesus has given him, i.e., testifying about the gospel of God's grace (20:24).

Paul's Strategies in Preaching the Gospel

Paul apprehends fully the importance of his commission, preaching the gospel, so that he could exclaim, "Woe to me if I do not preach the gospel!"[51] In this regard, Roland Allen's question, "how far was Paul's success due to his method of preaching?" is a relevant subject for missions research.[52] The following pages lay out Paul's strategies in preaching the gospel: (1) the contents of Paul's preaching, (2) Paul's attitude towards other religions, (3) Paul's method in dealing with other religions, and (4) the character of Paul's preaching.

---

[50]Phillips, 180. Paul, as a rabbi, was brought up on the traditional Jewish concept that a rabbi ought to be master of a secular trade. Phillips suggests it is a good idea that a Christian worker to do secular work once in a while because it helps remind the worker what it is like in the real workaday world. R. Sklba notes that Paul appears as a man of character, a man of prayer, a community member, a witness of the resurrection, an agent of conversion and change, a servant of the community, and a colleague in suffering. Therefore, Paul is a good model for diocesan priests today ("Paul of Tarsus: A Model for Diocesan Priesthood," *Emmanuel* 104 [August 1998]: 453-64). See also A. D. Clarke, "'Be Imitatiors of Me': Paul's Model of Leadership," *Tyndale Bulletin* 49 (February 1998): 329-60.

[51]1 Cor 9:16. Preaching is at the heart of Christianity because it has been the chief means of imparting the saving truths. Preaching conveys and explains the saving truths, and helps Christians keep on growing. The task of preaching the gospel is a peculiar job of a preacher. The preacher is the only one who is in the position to deal with the greatest need of the world. See George E. Sweazey, *Preaching the Good News* (Englewood Cliffs, NJ: Prentice-Hall, Inc., 1976), 6. Alfred Ernest Garvie introduces the ideas of Reformers toward the preaching ministry. He cites, "John Knox in the *Scots Confession* in 1560 which declares, 'The notes of the true Kirk of God, we believe, confess, and avow to be - First, the true preaching of the Word of God, in the which God has revealed Himself to us.' . . . In the *Augsburg Confession* in 1530, Luther and the Saxon Reformers defined the Church to be 'the congregation of saints (or general assembly of the faithful) wherein the Gospel is rightly taught and the Sacraments are rightly administered'" (*The Christian Preacher* [New York: Charles Scribner's Sons, 1928], 1-2). D. Martyn Lloyd-Jones seems to overestimate the preaching in the church. He notes that "preaching is the primary task of the Church and therefore of the minister of the Church, that everything else is subsidiary to this, and can be represented as the outworking or the carrying out of this in daily practice" (*Preaching and Preachers* [Grand Rapids, MI: Zondervan Publishing House, 1971], 26).

[52]Allen, 39.

The Contents of Paul's Preaching

Throughout his missionary career, Paul preaches the gospel to both the Jews and the Gentiles. He preaches the gospel in the synagogue, in Christian gatherings, in the plaza, in a private house, and in the marketplace. In this section, the following parts will be discussed: the subject of Paul's preaching, the structure of Paul's preaching, and the instance of Paul's preaching.

The Subject of Paul's Preaching

Paul makes his position clear to preach Christ-centered messages. In Athens, he preaches the good news about Jesus and the resurrection in the synagogues and in the marketplace (17:17-18). At the meeting of the Areopagus, Paul opens his message by responding to the Gentile gods and concludes with Jesus and his resurrection (17:22-32). When the ruler of the synagogue in Pisidian Antioch invites Paul to speak, Paul tries to prove that Jesus is the Messiah who is foretold in the Law and the Prophets (13:15-41). For both the Jews and the Gentiles, Paul preaches that Jesus is the only reconciler between God and human beings. His unique message about Jesus shocks both Jews and Gentiles. For the Jews, he goes beyond the boundary of the Jewish dimension of salvation; for the Gentiles, he dismisses other deities.[53] Consequently, the uniqueness of Paul's message leads to his unceasing hardships, persecutions, and spiritual warfare.[54] To him, Jesus Christ is the beginning and the end of his message. He thus, regards his missionary work as the continuing ministry of Jesus Christ.[55]

The Structure of Paul's Preaching

Most of Paul's messages have the following three parts: (1) the history of Israel as the divinely ordered preparation for the new revelation in the Messiah, (2) Jesus Christ

---

[53]Ho-Jin Chun, *Religious Pluralism and Mission Strategy for Other Religions* (Seoul: The Korea Society of Reformed Faith and Conduct, 1992), 81. Roger E. Hedlund analyzes the major subjects of Paul's message that appear repetitively in Paul's epistles as follows: the lostness of all men outside of Christ, the Lordship of Christ, redemption through Christ's death, justification by faith only, new life in Christ, reconciliation, the church, salvation of the Gentiles, law and grace, suffering, and the Christian hope (*The Mission of the Church in the World: A Biblical Theology* [Grand Rapids, MI: Baker Book House, 1985], 220).

[54]Harold Lindsell, *An Evangelical Theology of Missions* (Grand Rapids, MI: Zondervan Publishing House, 1970), 87-91. See also, John Dawson, *Taking Our Cities for God: How to Break Spiritual Strongholds* (Lake Mary, FL: Creation House, 1989), 133-37.

[55]Peter Beyerhaus, *Shaken Foundation: Theological Foundations for Mission* (Grand Rapids, MI: Zondervan Publishing House, 1972), 38. See also M. Clark, "St. Paul the Preacher," *Homiletic and Pastoral Review* 92 (March, 1991): 31-32, 51. Clark claims that "Paul reflected on the word of God and preached it in a living, dynamic, and intelligible way. Whoever, before and now, does not preach Christ crucified does not preach Christianity." See also G. Shillington, "Paul's Success in the Conversion of Gentiles: Dynamic Center in Cultural Diversity," *Direction* 20 (February 1991): 125-34.

as the promised Messiah who fulfilled the prophecies of the Old Testament, and (3) God's pardon for all who receive Jesus as the Savior and a solemn warning of punishment for all who reject Jesus as the Savior.[56] The same themes echo in Paul's preaching in Antioch of Pisidia (13:16-41), in Athens (17:22-31), and two interrupted sermonic addresses: one on the steps of the temple in Jerusalem speaking in Aramaic (22:1-23), and another in front of Agrippa and Festus (26:1-32). No one message, however, includes the whole contents. Yet all of his messages express the central element of the truth of Jesus Christ. In many instances, Paul emphasizes the death and resurrection of Jesus (13:27-37; 17:18, 31-32; 22:8; 26:23), but does not mention the life and ministry of Christ.[57]

Paul's Attitude towards Other Religions

Paul's declaration of the gospel in the face of opposing world religions is extremely strong and his writings are thoroughly logical. He burns with righteous indignation to see that Athens is full of idols, yet he refrained his anger and captured the moment as a contact point (17:16, 22). This section discusses Paul's both stern and modest stances in relation to other religious traditions.

Paul's Stern Stance towards Other Religions

---

[56]Jesse Burton Weatherspoon reviews Paul's message and notes the elements of his message as follows: (1) the age of the Messiah had come. The time of which the prophets predicted is fulfilled; (2) this fulfillment was realized in Jesus. He is the Messiah of Jewish hope. The Redeemer came to save the world to the life and freedom of the kingdom of God; and (3) on the basis of these facts and sure of hope, if men repent and be baptized in His name, the blessings of salvation would be theirs (*Sent Forth to Preach* [New York: Harper & Brothers, 1954], 81-101). Paul Scott Wilson cites four parts of Paul's message: (1) the usual pattern included an introduction; (2) a narration or summary of the relevant events including a clear statement of the issue, basic facts, the thesis and one's rationale; (3) the argument or proof divided into parts, which was the main body of the speech and included arguments for and against one's position; and (4) a

conclusion (*A Concise History of Preaching* [Nashville, T: Abingdon Press, 1992], 25). Don N. Howell Jr. presents four elements of Paul's preaching as follows: (1) the essential difference between idols and the one true and living God (theology proper); (2) the death and resurrection of Jesus, the Son of God (Christology); (3) the return of Jesus to judge (God's wrath) unbelievers and rescue his people (soteriology/eschatology); and (4) an appeal to "turn" (repentance) from idols and to "serve" (faith/obedience) the living God ("Mission in Paul's Epistles: Genesis, Pattern, and Dynamics," in *Mission in the New Testament: An Evangelical Approach*, ed. William J. Larkin Jr. and Joel F. Williams [Maryknoll, NY: Orbis Books, 1998], 71).

[57]C. H. Dodd notes, "It would be rash to argue from silence that Paul ignored the life of Jesus in his preaching; for, as we have seen, that preaching is represented only fragmentarily, and as it were accidentally, in the epistles. That he was aware of the historical life of Jesus, and cited His sayings as authoritative need not be shown over again. It may be, for all we know, that the brief recital of historical facts in 1 Cor 15:1 *ff.* is only the conclusion of a general summary which may have included some reference to the ministry. But this remains uncertain." (*The Apostolic Preaching and Its Developments* [New York: Harper & Brothers, Publishers, 1960], 28-29).

Paul's basic stance on the gospel is absolute. He does not compromise in his declaration of Christ even within Judaism in which he grew up and where part of theChristian message originates (13:39; 15:1-2). No matter how severe his persecutions are, Paul refuses to change his attitude towards other religions (14:22; 21:13). He rejects all idols. When the priest of Zeus in Lystra, for instance, attempts to worship Paul and Barnabas, Paul urges the people to turn from worthless worshiping idols to the worship of the living God (14:15). In Athens, Paul repudiates any attempt of a deity made of gold, silver, or stone (17:29).[58]

Paul's Modest Stance towards Other Religions

Although Paul denounces idolatry in strongest terms, he makes no bitter and virulent attacks upon his hearers. In Ephesus, for instance, when a number of sorcerers burn their books publicly, as a result of his preaching, Paul experiences no fierce reaction from the public (19:19). Evidently, Paul would use strong arguments to persuade his hearers, but does not employ abrasive language that would invite the ire of the adherents of world religions. When a silversmith named Demetrius and other silver traders of shrines of Artemis led the whole Ephesus in an uproar, the address of the city clerk of Ephesus to the mob in the theater testifies that Paul and his team have neither robbed temples nor blasphemed the goddess of Ephesus (19:37). As Hendrik Kramer observes, Paul's attitude towards the non-Christian religions is a remarkable combination of downright intrepidity and of radical humility.[59]

Paul's Methods in Dealing with Other Religions

Paul preaches the gospel to hearts that are spiritually needy. This would sometimes invite the ire of world religions. Paul collides with Judaism in Pisidian Antioch and Thessalonica (13:13-52; 17: 5-10), faces idolatrous systems in Lystra (14:8-18), and disputes with Hellenism in Athen (17:16-34). All these non Judeo-Christian religious traditions are highly developed, well organized, and heavily influential to people throughout the Roman Empire.[60] To preach the gospel in this hostile environment, Paul would develop appropriate missions strategies especially when the proclamation of the gospel is concerned. Paul then adapts the following methods for contacting different people: using the Scripture, engaging in power

---

[58]Paul's attitude toward other religions in his epistles are as follows: (1) they are "dead in transgressions and sins" (Eph 2:1); (2) they are blind (2 Cor 4:4); (3) "they are darkened in their understanding and separated from the life of God." (Eph 4:18); (4) they are in darkness (Eph 5:8).

[59]Hendrik Kraemer, *The Christian Message in a Non-Christian World* (Grand Rapids, MI: Kregel Publications, 1977), 128.

[60]For further discussion about Paul's ministry and Greco-Roman society, see E. Earle Ellis, *Pauline Theology* (Grand Rapids, MI: William B. Eerdmans Publishing Company, 1989), 147-59.

conflict, and creating contact point.[61]

Using the Scriptures

To approach people in the Jewish synagogue, Paul makes it his custom to visit synagogue in every city he enters (17:2). As a highly qualified teacher and rabbi trained under Gamaliel, the rulers of synagogue often invites him to admonish the people (13:15; 22:3). Paul would begin by unfolding the message from the Law of Moses and Prophets to Jesus Christ. He would move on to argue that Jesus is the Messiah whom the Scriptures promised (13:16-43). The use of Scriptures to prove his point is appropriate to people who belong to the covenant system, the Jews.

Engaging in Power Conflict

Paul's missionary work is beset with power conflicts.[62] In Paphos, for instance, he makes Bar-Jesus, a Jewish sorcerer and false prophet, blind because the sorcerer tries to turn the proconsul, Sergius Paulus, from the faith (13:6-11). Paul heals a crippled man in Lystra (14:8-10). He casts out a spirit from a demon-possessed slave girl in Philippi (16:18), and cures many sick persons and casts out evil spirits, even the sick who were touched by handkerchiefs and aprons from him were cured (19:11-12).[63] In Ephesus, a number of sorcerers bring their scrolls together and burned them publicly because they experience the power of the Holy Spirit through Paul (19:19). Obviously, people accept the gospel as Paul demonstrates its power through miraculous signs, healing, and deliverance from evil spirits (13:12; 14:21-23; 19:17-20; 28:5, 8-9).

Creating Contact Point

In the Hellenistic society that has a little or no prior knowledge of Christian ideas, Paul uses a different approach in sharing the good news. In Athens, for instance, while dealing with

---

[61] Jun, *Missiology*, 197. See also 1 Cor 9:20-23.

[62] Dennis E. Johnson interprets the power conflict in Acts as follows: "As the word of Jesus confronts the Greco-Roman world's religions, a theme from the prophecy of Isaiah finds fulfillment: The Lord is filing a lawsuit against the hollow gods in which the Gentiles trust, proving the idols guilty of false advertising for having claimed that they can rescue their worshippers. The idols can present no witnesses to attest their claims, but the Lord subpoenas his servant Israel to testify to his power to save... God's truth confronts humanity's religions. His redemptive acts in history refute the myths invented by human imagination and speculation. Through the words of his witness-bearing church, Christ the risen Lord extends his arms to fugitives who have sought refuge from life's assaults in idols of wood or images of the mind" (*The Message of Acts in the History of Redemption* [Phillipsburg, NJ: P & R Publishing Company, 1997], 169).

[63] T. J. Leary, "The 'Aprons' of St. Paul-Acts 19:12," *Journal of Theological Studies* 41 (February 1990): 527-29. Leary asserts that Paul's apron was not a specialist garment that some commentators connect it with Paul's leather-working, but something worn generally use a "belt."

local philosophers on Mars Hill, Paul establishes a contact point by utilizing symbols from people's culture and religion. This he does complimenting the Athenians on their religiosity, arousing their curiosity, and creating an interest to listen to what he is telling them (17:16-31).[64] He utilizes the symbol of "an unknown God,"(17: 23) and maximizes it in his preaching in Athens. The local symbol allows Paul to create a suitable contact point, a key to his gospel presentation. Theologically speaking, Paul seems to recognize the Gentiles as potential heirs of the promise of God.[65]

The Character of Paul's Preaching

The preaching of God's Word highlights Paul's missionary work. He distinguishes himself from other preachers who are peddling the word of God.[66] Paul strives to present the truth and avoid obscuring the message of God (20:27). Thus, the following pages will show the character of Paul's message in terms of its clarity, persuasion, urgency, Bible-orientation, and contextualization.

<u>The Message is Clear</u>

Paul presents his hearers a clear and definite understanding of what is required of them in his preaching. He is forthright in dealing with idolatry, debunking any notion that all religious worship is a worship of the true God, and that all world religions lead to the same God (16:31; 17:30; 18:5; 20:21). The clarity of his message separates those who accept the message from the rejecters.[67] To new believers, Paul presents the hardship that they will face, in that they are expected to endure as members of the kingdom of God (14:22). In Miletus, Paul declares that he has not hesitated to preach anything that would help people in following Christ (20:20).

---

[64]Hedlund, 222-25. See also Karl Olav Sandnes, "Paul and Socrates: The Aim of Paul's Areopagus Speech," *Journal for the Study of the New Testament* 50 (June 1993): 17-20. See also P. Sciberras, "The Figure of Paul in the Acts of the Apostles. The Areopagos Speech," *Melita Theologica* 43 (January 1992): 1-15.

[65]J. H. Bavink consents that Paul saw something, contact point, which reflected, however dimly, mankind's quest for God in the inscription to the "unknown God" at Athens. Paul, however, also saw the human tendency to push God gradually out of our lives and to fill the vacuum with other beings, "spirits and souls, saints and magic, and alien interests" (*An Introduction to the Science of Missions,* trans. D. H. Freeman [Grand Rapids, MI: Baker Book House, 1960], 260). John T. Seamands presents three acceptable contact points: (1) the universal need for forgiveness, the universal hunger for fellowship with God- the gospel as a universal faith has universal application to the fundamental needs of people; (2) common interests, common needs and problems, and common religious ideas-something common can be a starting point in presenting the gospel; (3) antithesis between the gospel and the world religions-some conflicting pointcan be the contact point (*Tell It Well: Communicating the Gospel Across Cultures* [Kansas City, MO: Beacon Hill Press of Kansas City, 1981], 79-88).

[66]2 Cor 2:17; 4:2.

[67]See Acts 13:43-45; 14:4; 17:4-5; 18:5-8; 19:9; 22:22; 23:9; 28:24.

The Message is Persuasive

Persuasion characterizes Paul's preaching. He strives to bring his hearers speedily and directly to a point of decision, and urges them to make a choice and act upon such choice (26:20). In Lystra, for example, Paul instructs the priest of Zeus to turn immediately from the worthless things to the living God (14:15). Whenever he reaches the point of making a decision, Paul would persuade listeners to surrender themselves to the Lord, by renouncing the past and turn to Jesus Christ (17:30-31). He makes people clear that the Christian message is not simply a story to tell and hear, but a life to live out.

The Message is Urgent

Urgency marks Paul's preaching ministry. He preaches the word of God to people who would listen to and accept it, but leaves quickly when turned down. A good case in point is Pisidian Antioch, where people expels Paul and Barnabas from the region. In response to the hostile act, the two apostles shake the dust from their feet and decide to go to other city (13:51).

The Message is Scriptural

The Law of Moses and the Prophets are crucial foundations to Paul's messages. Preaching in a synagogue in Pisidian Antioch, Paul appeals to the history of Israel from Exodus to Jesus Christ (13: 17-41). He also preaches from the Scriptures for three Sabbath days in a synagogue in Thessalonica (17:2). Influenced by Paul's teaching, believers in Berea would examine the Scriptures seriously and daily (17:11). Even in a Roman prison, Paul preaches about the resurrected Jesus and the kingdom of God citing the Law of Moses and the Prophets (28:23, 30-31). Clearly enough Paul's preaching remains Scriptural knowing that new believers need a firm foundation on God's word.[68]

The Message is Contextualized

The use of relevant symbols and categories that are available in a local is critical to Paul's preaching ministry. In his synagogue preaching, Paul would normally start his message from the Old Testament so the Jews and the Gentile God-fearers could identify with him (13:17; 14:1; 17:1-3, 10; 18:4, 19; 19:8). In one instance, a priest of

---

[68]Delos Miles emphasizes the importance of the Bible-based message through an interpretation of 1 Cor 15:3-5. He notes, "Christ died for our sins in accordance with Scriptures" (Introduction to Evangelism [Nashville, TN: Broadman Press, 1983], 62).

Zeus in Lystra attempts to offer sacrifices to Paul, but this was immediately corrected as Paul seizes the moment and turns it into an opportunity to preach about the living God (14:13-15). He uses the theme of suffering after getting up from being knock down unconscious as a result from the stoning of the Jews in Lystra (14:19-22). He takes advantage of the environment in prison in Philippi to present the gospel to the jailer and his household (16:25-34). He cites an "unknown god" in Athens to introduce people to the one and living God (17:23). Paul also would quote a passage from the Greek poem to make his message more relevant, acceptable, and understandable (17: 28).[69] All of these efforts contribute to Paul's success in contextualizing his message.

Paul's Strategies in Equipping Leaders

The most urgent need of the newly planted church is not her building, programs, or any equipment, but leaders.[70] Paul's missionary activities show a careful and deliberate system of equipping elders for the local church leadership. The following pages will show (1) the status of local leadership in Pauline churches, (2) the qualifications for leadership, (3) the foundations of leadership and (4) the methods of training leadership evaded in the churches that Paul planted.

The Status of Local Leadership in Pauline Churches

Paul gives great attention to training and equipping leaders, both men and women, in local churches. He considers local leaders as "co-laborers in Christ." Local leadership, in this regard, roots in divine guidance, synagogue tradition, and women leadership.

---

[69] Albert Barnes, *Notes on the New Testament: Acts*, ed. Robert Frew (London: Blackie and Son, 1885; reprint, Grand Rapids, MI: Baker Books, 1998), 264.

[70] David J. Hesselgrave emphasizes the importance of leadership. He notes that it is common for church-planters to desire that groups of new believers organize as soon as practicable. No organization can be stronger than its leadership. Therefore, to think, pray, work, and plan with a view to rising up spiritual leadership for the organizing church should be of first priority. When spiritual leadership emerges, organization will become practicable and essential (Planting Churches Cross-Culturally: A Guide for Home and Foreign Missions [Grand Rapids, MI: Baker Book House, 1980], 349). Byung-Yoon Kim stresses that developing effective pastoral leadership is one of the most important responsibilities of the church planter especially when one is a foreign missionary ("An Analysis of the Church Planting Methods of Korean Evangelical Missionaries in the Philippines" [Th.D. diss., Asia Baptist Graduate Theological Seminary, 1998], 69). Samuel D. Faircloth presents the meaning of leadership after his studies of three Greek words. He notes that "the Greek vocabulary for leader or leadership in Rom 12:8 (προισητμι), 1 Cor 12:28 (κυβερνησις), and Heb 13:7, 17, 24 (ἡγεομαι), we find that this gift enables a leader to superintend, preside, govern, administer, command, and rule or lead. The possession of this gift gives a person an overwhelming sense of mission-an inner spiritual drive toward his goals" (Church Planting for Reproduction [Grand Rapids, MI: Baker Book House, 1991], 100).

Divine Guidance

The book of Acts evidences that the Holy Spirit is directly involved in the selecting, equipping, and commissioning of local church leaders.[71] The Holy Spirit initiates Paul's missions works. Paul and Barnabas receive their ministry appointments from the Holy Spirit, with the support of the church in Antioch (13:1-3). Paul and other apostles would discover soon the necessity of appointing leaders and elders. This they do by prayer and fasting and selecting those leaders (13:2; 14:23). The Holy Spirit initiates the process of appointing local leaders. In Philippi, for instance, Lydia responded to Paul and accepts the gospel by the initiatory work of the Holy Spirit and become the leader of the church (16:14). The Holy Spirit encouraged Paul to continue his ministry in Corinth longer (18:9-10), and apparently he would equip many leaders like Titus Justus, Crispus, and Aquila and Priscilla (18: 2, 7-8). The Holy Spirit expedites Paul's ministries.[72] In Paphos, the proconsul, Sergius Paulus believes the Lord when he experienced the power of the Holy Spirit through Paul who makes Elymas, a Jewish sorcerer and false prophet who tries to turn the proconsul from the faith, blind (13:11-12). Likewise, Paul's miracles enabled by the Holy Spirit accelerate the advance of the gospel greatly (14:21; 16:32-34; 19:17-20; 28:5-10). The Holy Spirit completes Paul's ministries. Paul acknowledges his limitations so that he commits his ministries to the caring ministry of the Holy Spirit. He recognizes that his contribution to missions would simply be the planting of the seed. The Holy Spirit, however, makes it grow.[73] In Pisidian region and Ephesus, for instance, Paul appoints elders in each church and he commits them to the Holy Spirit and to the word of His grace (14:23; 20:32). By doing this, he emphasizes the work of the Holy Spirit rather than the work of human tools.

Synagogue Tradition

Most converts of the early church have some Judaic background, which combine temple and synagogues system.[74] It is natural for these new believers to follow the

---

[71]J. N. Suggit, " 'The Holy Spirit and We resolved …'(Acts 15:28)," *Journal of Theology for Southern Africa* 79 (1992): 38-48. Suggit insists that the work of the Holy Spirit cannot be separated from the institutional structures of the church. See also Orlando E. Costas, The Integrity of Mission: The Inner Life and Outreach of the Church (New York, NY: Harper & Row, 1979), 27.

[72]John R. W. Stott, "The Living God Is a Missionary God," in *Perspectives on the World Christian Movement*, ed., Ralph D. Winter and Steven C. Hawthorne (Pasadena, CA: William Carey Library, 1992), A-18.

[73]1 Cor 3:6; See also Joseph Jung-Yeol Chang, *Missions And Church Growth* (Seoul: Sung Kwang Publishing Co., 1978), 71.

[74]In synagogue, to organize a synagogue or hold meetings, at least ten men are necessary. The elders of the congregations select ruler(s) among themselves. The ruler has the responsibilities for synagogue

synagogue traditions and patterns of organization because Paul is silent on the specific structure of church organization, worship order, church program, or any liturgy.[75] Even if the early church believers find a model for church leadership and organization in the synagogue, they do not seem to follow the synagogue pattern rigidly. Yet, the early believers could be aware of the basics for conducting corporate spiritual life and business.

Women Leadership

In the Jewish and Hellenistic society, men view women as having a subordinate status to man according to which women are inferior and therefore have limited rights. Paul daringly challenges such un-Scriptural old fixed ideas and incites women to participate in ministry.[76] Paul seems to be the first who actively encourages women to practice leadership in the church. Lydia is the first Christian in Europe and leader of the first church in Europe under Paul's leadership (16:13-15).[77] Priscilla and Aquila would become the leading figure in Corinthian church.[78] They seem to learn the Bible

---

services and properties. The ruler often designates others to conduct the expressions of praise, prayers, readings of the Law and the Prophets, and the giving of exhortations. Several assistants carry out menial duties, inflict corporal punishment or otherwise disciplined members, and dispense alms received from the members (C. L. Feinberg, "Synagogue," in J. D. Douglas, gen. ed., *The New Bible Dictionary* [Grand Rapids, MI: William Eerdmans Publishing Company, 1962], 1227-29).

[75]Thomson finds principles in Acts 20:7; 1 Cor 11:23-28; Eph 5:19; and Col 3:16. He writes, "Worship was conducted in believers' home. Official ministrants would be unnecessary. Simplicity would be the keynote of these house-church worship services, consisting for the most part of praise, prayer, reading from the Scriptures, and exposition. The love feast, followed by the Lord's Supper, were also common features of Christian worship. But the emphasis throughout would be upon the Spirit, and the inner love and devotion of the heart" (R.V.G. Thomson, "Worship," in J. D. Douglas, gen. ed., *The New Bible Dictionary* [Grand Rapids, MI: William B. Eerdmans Publishing Co., 1962], 1340). See also Hesselgrave, 314-18.

[76]Pamela Eisenbaum asserts, "Paul is an ally of Christian conservatives who wish to keep women in a subordinate position to men" ("Is Paul the Father of Misogyny and Antisemitism?" *Cross Current* 50 [Winter 2000-2001]: 506). N. Guillemette, "Saint Paul and Women," *East Asia Pastoral Review* 26 (February 1989): 121-33. Guillemette claims that the error of those who accuse Paul of misogyny is their failure to take into account his cultural background. James D. G. Dunn notes, "So far as the ministry of women in the Pauline churches is concerned the position could hardly be clearer. Women were prominent in ministry. If we simply take the final chapter of our principal text, Rom 16, the point is made for us. There we meet first of all Phoebe (16.1-2), who is described as both a 'deacon' and a 'patron' of the church in Cenchreae. Phoebe, indeed, is the first person within Christian history to be named 'deacon'" (*The Theology of Paul the Apostle* [Grand Rapids, MI: William B. Eerdmans Publishing Company, 1998], 586-87). See also Ivoni Richter Reimer, *Women in the Acts of the Apostles*, trans. Linda M. Maloney (Minneapolis, MN: Fortress Press, 1995), 252.

[77]John Temple Bristow, *What Paul Really Said about Women* (San Francisco: Harper and Row, 1988), 55.

[78]D. J. Doughty, "Luke's Story of Paul in Corinth: Fictional History in Acts 18," *Journal of Higher Criticism* 4 (January 1997): 3-54. Doughty criticizes that Luke's depiction of Paul as the founder of the Christian community in Corinth in Acts 18 is an imaginative apologetic rewriting of earlier traditions

in depth from Paul and they instruct Apollos regarding the right doctrines (18:26). Luke notes that there are a number of prominent Greek women who believe the gospel (17:4, 12, 34; 21:9) and their influences are great.[79] Women usually open their homes as places of meetings and this service leads to the establishment of permanent churches. Women take places of responsibility in the churches and acquit themselves.[80] Mobilizing women for the service of the Lord is one of the eminences of Paul's missions strategies.

The Qualifications for Leadership

Roland Allen observes that modern missionaries gather in large numbers, but they could hardly train people to maintain their own spiritual life. Paul would preach in a place between five to six months, and then leaves behind him a church and trained leaders.[81] The choosing and appointing of local leadership in a young church is critical to Paul's missions strategies. The following pages will show the qualifications for leadership in terms of proven leaders and local leaders.

---

having quite different views of Christian beginnings in Corinth.

[79]Sang-Keun Lee, *The Acts of the Apostles* (Seoul: The Department of Education of the General Assembly of the Korean Presbyterian Church, 1983), 200. See also J. Rook, "Women in Acts: Are They Equal Partner with Men in the Earliest Church?" McMaster Journal of Theology 2 (February 1991): 29-41. Rook examines the question whether women were equal to men in status and ministerial function in the early church according to Acts. Women are prominence, wealth, and respect. Nevertheless, women are not depicted as participating in major decision, even when these directly affect women. In Acts the common patriarchal views of the first century remain intact.

[80]John Temple Bristow argues that women practiced equally the same responsibility with men to serve the Lord in the early church as follows: "Although Paul did not establish the practice of having women lead in worship alongside men, he certainly did approve of it." Bristow presents Peter's sermon on the Day of Pentecost as the base of his assertion. He says that "when God pours out His Spirit on all flesh, it is said, 'your sons and your daughters shall prophesy' (Joel 2:28-32). It would be strange, indeed, if the Church under the apostles regarded the Day of Pentecost as a sign of the new age in Christ and yet forbade women the right to give inspired messages to the Church! Certainly, women exercised the gift of prophecy in the age of Paul" (Bristow, 57-58). R.T.France also argues that 1 Tim. 2:8-15 is not universal regulation; it is Paul's instruction for Timothy how to lead the Ephesian church. Therefore, the passages concerning for woman leadership must be limited in Ephesian situation only, not the rest of the New Testament Church (*Women in the Church's Ministry: A Test-case for Biblical Hermeneutics* [Cumbria, UK: The Paternoster Press, 1995], 69-72). Don Williams insists that the reason why there is no ordination of women in the New Testament is that there was no clergy-laity distinction; there was only a distinction in gifts. Williams concludes that since women as well as men are gifted for ministry, they must be allowed to use their gifts (*The Apostle Paul and Women in the Church* [Ventura, CA: Regal Books, 1982,], 145-7). John Meyendorff presents five points of the negative reaction of the Orthodox Church to the idea of ordaining women to the sacramental priesthood (*Witness to the World* [Crestwood, NY: St. Vladimir's Seminary Press], 54-8). See also Judith M. Gundry-Volf, "Paul on Women and Gender: A Comparison with Early Jewish Views," in *The Road from Damascus: The Impact of Paul's Conversion on His Life, Thought, and Ministry*, ed. Richard N. Longenecker (Grand Rapids, MI: William B. Eerdmans Publishing Company, 1997), 186. See also C. A. Anderson Scott, *Christianity According to St. Paul* (London: Cambridge University Press, 1966), 228.

[81]Allen, 79.

Proven Leaders

The church must choose its leaders among proven people before leaders are appointed. When the Holy Spirit calls out Paul and Barnabas as church planters, He selects the two most proven, experienced, fruitful disciple makers in Antioch church (13:1-3).[82] It is possible for a recognized social leader to become a good spiritual leader of the newly planted church if the person is truly converted and consecrated to God. Thus, Paul maximizes his opportunities to reach the people of high standing and respected leaders in their community (13:6-12; 17:4, 12, 18; 18:8; 26:28-30; 28:8, 17).[83] Paul chooses Timothy as one of his missionary team members because of Timothy's good reputation not only those in the place where he was born, but also those in the neighboring cities (16:1-5).[84]

Local Leaders

After preaching the gospel and planting a church in a place, it is natural for Paul to build up the leadership and appoint elders among the local people (14:23; 20:17). Although the indigenous leadership system is not original in Paul's churches (11:30; 15:2), Paul maximizes this system for his newly planted churches. He understands the power of local leadership, as he himself is an indigenous missionary, coming from Tarsus of Cilicia (22:3) and holds a Roman citizenship (22:28). His indigenous roots provide opportunities to advance the gospel in the Gentile area (16:37-40; 22:29; 25:11). Paul chooses Timothy as one of his missionary team members not only because of the latter's good reputation, but also due to indigenous origins (16:1-5).[85] In Macedonia, Paul adds Luke, a local person, to his missionary team (16:9).[86] Eventually, Paul chooses elders in each church, he chooses them from the local congregation, thus, ruling out outsiders to serve as an elder of a local church. Paul seems to understand the advantage of local people and to maximize it in his ministries.

---

[82]Paul Kaak, "Provenness," *Evangelical Missions Quarterly* 34 (April 1998): 165.

[83]Larry Pate, *Starting New Churches* (Brussels: International Correspondence Institute, 1978), 152. Pate notes that, "in every village and every area of town or city, there are people who are recognized as leaders. They are recognized leaders because the people respect their opinions and value their judgments. When there is a local argument, the people come to these leaders to settle it. When a representative is needed to speak to officials, the recognized leader will be asked to speak for the people. When something new happens in the area, the people come to these leaders to see what they think about it."

[84]See 1 Tim. 3:7. When Paul admonishes Timothy how to choose leaders in the church, he instructed Timothy to select "a good reputation with outsiders."

[85]Matthew Henry, *Commentary on the Whole Bible*, vol. 6, *Acts to Revelation* (Old Tappan, NJ: Fleming H. Revell Company, n.d.), 202.

[86]Yune-Sun Park, *A Commentary on the Book of the Acts* (Seoul: Yung Eum Sa, 1981), 17, 338.

The Foundations of Leadership Training

The future of every church depends on the quality of the leaders it produces. In this sense, M. L. Hodge points out that nothing may be more important than the preparation of its future leadership in the church life.[87] Paul understands this aspect so well that he appoints leaders in every church that he has planted as soon as possible. In training leadership, Paul has three foundations: the doctrinal, the practical, and spiritual foundation.

The Doctrinal Foundation of Leadership

Paul teaches his converts the essence of the Christian doctrine: God the Father as Creator, Jesus Christ as the Redeemer and Savior, and the Holy Spirit.[88] Beside these basic doctrines, Paul leaves a tradition that is called the apostolic decree reached by the apostles and elders in Jerusalem (15:28-29, 31; 16:4).[89] He teaches the Old Testament from which he argues that Jesus is the Messiah for the whole world (17:2-3; 18:5, 28). Although the Old Testament is originally the peculiar property of the Jews, Paul strives to make it universal. He reminds local leaders of their calling of the Holy Spirit and the task to protect their congregation from the attack of Satan (20:26-31).

The Practical Foundation of Leadership

Paul teaches leaders of the church to exemplify the Christian life. In Lystra, he admonishes Christians to be prepared to go through many hardships as they enter the kingdom of God (14:19-22; 20:19). He teaches leaders prayer and fasting, especially when a church decides on matters related to their lives and ministries (13:2; 14:23). He teaches leaders how to entrust things that are beyond their control to the Lord. In so doing, Paul commits the church and the leaders of the church to the Lord (14:23; 20:32, 36). Other essentials of Christian life Paul teaches include purity, stewardship, compassion for ministry (20:32-35), and a sacrificial life for the Lord by word and deed (20:22-24; 21:13).

The Spiritual Foundation of Leadership

---

[87]M. L. Hodges, *A Guide to Church Planting* (Chicago: Moody Press, 1973), 78.

[88]See Acts 13:16-41; 14:15-17; 16:31; 17:24-33; 18:5; 19:2-7; 20:21; 28:31.

[89]Bruce, *The Book of the Acts,* 305. See also William Sanford LaSor, *Church Alive: A Bible Commentary for Laymen: Acts* (Glendale, CA: Regal Books, 1952), 246-47. In his epistles, Paul constantly refers to the tradition and teachings of the apostolic decree (1 Cor 11:2, 23; 2 Thess 2:15; 3:6; 1 Tim 6:20; 2 Tim 1:13; 2:2; 3:14).

One of Paul's strategies for training his new converts to stand firm and grow into maturity is that he trusts that the Holy Spirit will continue the remaining ministries.[90] He commits the churches to the Holy Spirit and goes to another place even if the churches need more guidance (Acts 14: 23; 20:32). Paul's longest stay in one place is eighteen months in Corinth (18:11), and three years in Ephesus (20:31). In other places Paul stays a few weeks or months. These periods are considerably short for equipping leaders properly. However, Paul entrusts them to the Holy Spirit and leaves for other places. Paul expects the human being's natural capabilities of growth and expansion. Since most of the leaders are proven people and have Judaic background or knowledge of the Old Testament, Paul seems to trust their capabilities to be good leaders through the equipping ministry of the Holy Spirit.[91] He usually moves to other place in the midst of revival (13:1-3). For instance, it is after a tremendous victory that Paul leaves the island of Cyprus to go to Perga (13:6-13). In Ephesus, Paul leaves for Jerusalem after a great revival (19:20). Likewise, Paul entrusts the leadership of the church to the hands of the local church leaders and of the Holy Spirit's sustaining grace.

The Methods of Training Leadership

Paul employs some strategies when he trains his new converts to stand firm and to grow into maturity. His methods of training are as follows: regular teaching of the Scriptures, formal institution, and reinforcement ministry.Regular Teaching of the Scriptures

Paul excells in teaching people as he teaches a great number of them in Antioch church before his missionary career (11:26). He teaches people the basic doctrines in the synagogues, on a regular basis. In Pisidian Antioch, for instance, Paul teaches people in the synagogue for two consecutive Sabbath days (13:15, 42-49). Paul and Barnabas teach a great number of Jews and Gentiles in the synagogue in Iconium (14:1) and for three Sabbath days in Thessalonica (17:2, 17). Paul's ministry in Berea, teaching the Scriptures everyday, seems to be a modern type of series Bible study (17:11). His teaching in Rome is the same type of regular series teaching (28:23).[92]

Formal Institution

Paul teaches the Scriptures in a formal institution. In Ephesus, for instance, he

---

[90]John 14:26. A. Edanad, "The Spirit and the Christian Community according to Acts of the Apostles," *Jeevadhara* 28 (1998): 98-108. Edanad describes how the Holy Spirit dynamically present, animating, inspiring, guiding, transforming, and strengthening the early Christian community in Acts.

[91]Lenski concludes that the elders in Pauline churches are all Jews. He argues that only the Jews have the sufficient knowledge of the Old Testament that is the basement of Christianity (85). However, there is no necessity to consent with Lenski on this point because there are many God-fearing prominent Gentiles in the synagogues and there is no evidence that they were prohibited to be elders in Pauline churches.

[92]Lenski, 491-503.

holds teaching sections in the synagogue for three months. After synagogue teaching, Paul teaches disciples in the lecture hall of Tyrannus daily for two years (19:8-9).

Reinforcement Ministry

Paul reinforces the leaders of the churches by his follow-up visitation. His usual ministry is to revisit the churches, to strengthen their souls, and to encourage them to continue in the faith (14:22). Through the reinforcement ministry, he trains and equips the leaders of the churches appropriately for the service of the Lord (15:36; 16:40;18:22-23; 20:1-2, 17-38). Paul occasionally lets other team members revisit the churches, resolve the current problem of the churches, and reinforce the leaders (19:22).

Paul's Strategies in Financing the Ministry

Financial matter is the *sine qua non* of every aspect of human lives from the cradle to the grave.[93] Church finances, however, are not mentioned often in Acts. Although Paul actually needs money for traveling widely and supporting his missions team members, and actually transacts money (21:24-26; 28:30), he seems to consider money of less importance and does not depend upon financial aid from others. Financial arrangement often affects the relationship between missionary and those who are near to the missionary seriously.[94] This section, therefore, discusses the issue of a self-support missionary and self-supporting church.

Self-Supporting Missionary

Paul is a self-supporting missionary. He does not normally seek financial help for himself; rather he supports himself and his colleagues by working with his own hands. Paul is a tentmaker, and from this trade he supports his missions team often (Acts 18:3; 20:34).[95] In Paul's time, many teachers wander from town to town collecting money

---

[93]Herbert Kane points out some wrong presumptions about money as follows: (1) Money is not dirty, (2) Nothing is wrong with financial appeals, (3) Missionary is not a beggar, (4) All Christians should live by faith, (5) Living by faith has nothing to do with money per se (6) God does supply the needs of His servants (*Life and Work on the Mission Field* [Grand Rapids, MI: Baker Book House, 1980], 65-66).

[94]Paul comprehends fully the realities of money problems warning thus: "for the love of money is a root of all kinds of evil" (1 Tim. 6:10). See also Wade Coggins, "The Risks of Sending Our Dollar Only," *Evangelical Missions Quarterly* 24 (July 1988): 204-6.

[95]F. F. Bruce translates the Greek, 'σχηνοποιος' as 'saddler' or 'leather-worker.' Bruce writes, "Paul is a leather-worker by trade and this trade is closely connected with the principal manufacture of Paul's native province, a cloth of goat's hair called *cilicium,* used for making cloaks, curtains and so forth. A

from those who attend their lectures. He accepts those preachers and argues that it is legitimate.[96] Paul, however, keeps himself away from them (20:33). He tries to avoid becoming a financial burden to new believers. When Lydia, for instance, invites Paul and his missions team to stay in her house, she has to beg and constrain them, saying, "If you have judged me to be faithful to the Lord, come to my house and stay" (16:15).[97]

On the later part of his life, Paul seems to have had considerable resources. His last trip, for instance, with other team members (20:4) from Macedonia to Jerusalem takes a long time with high cost (20:6, 13-16; 21:1-3, 7-8, 15-17). Paul pays the expenses for the four men's purification rites in Jerusalem (21:24). Paul's long judicial process in the court of Felix, Festus, and Agrippa in Caesarea prison for more than two years requires high expenses, too (24:2, 23, 27; 25:13-27; 26;30). The fact that Paul gains a respectful hearing from provincial governors, and to excite their avarices may prove that he has some resources (24:24-27). From where Paul obtains such large supplies is not important; but even if he receives them from his converts, it is still consistent with his earlier practice.[98]

---

scribe or rabbi received no payment for his teaching, and many of them therefore practiced a trade in addition to their study and teaching of the law" (*The Book of the Acts,* 367-68).

[96] 1 Cor 9:7-12.

[97] William Hendrikson prepares Paul's ten presumable answers to the question, "whether a preacher of the gospel can collect payments from the converts," as follows: (1) Paul wants not to be one of those deceivers who "teach things they ought not to teach-and that for the sake of dishonest gain" (Titus 1:10-11), (2) Though Paul has the right to receive money even from his converts, he give up his right for the sake of his converts (1 Cor 9:7-15), (3) "I have not coveted anyone's silver or gold or clothing" (Acts 20:33), (4) Paul receives some supports from other existing church while he was preaching in a new place (2 Cor 11:8-9), (5) Paul receives some supports from the Philippian church (Phil 4:10-20), (6) Paul himself works night and day, laboring and toiling so that he and his companions would not be a burden to any of converts (Acts 20:34,35; 1 Thess 2:9; 2 Thess 3:8), (7) Paul is a tentmaker (Acts18:3), (8) Everything is permissible for Paul, but not everything is beneficial. He seeks the glory of God and His kingdom first (1 Cor 6:12; 8:9,13; 9:12-15), (9) Paul did not wants to give any clue to his opponents to ridicule him by taking some money from his converts (2 Cor 11:7-15), and (10) Paul declares an important principle, "If a man will not work, he shall not eat" (2 Thess 3:10). He estimates labor highly (*I & II Thessalonicans* [London: The Banner of Truth, 1972], 66).

[98] Allen, 45-51. Alvin Roy Snellar arranges Paul's fundamental attitudes toward financial matters as follows: (1) Paul, as a rabbi, collects no money from his audiences according to the rabbinical traditions. Paul learns the skill to make tents, and by which he supports his life and ministries, (2) Though preachers receive payments are common practice in his time, Paul refuses it because he wants not to be a burden to the church (Acts 20:33). By practicing it, Paul experiences the word of the Lord, "It is more blessed to give than to receive" (Acts 20:35), (3) Paul admonishes that "each one should remain in the situation which he is in when God calls him" (1 Cor 7:20). All people should consider their occupation as what God has given so that in and by their occupation they have to serve the Lord. God's blessing is not limited in a specific occupation. Paul, thus, continues to make tents, (4) Paul advocates that he has the right to receive payments by citing several texts from Scripture (1 Cor 9:14,20), However, by refusing this right, Paul let nobody suspects his motive for preaching the gospel. (5) Paul acknowledges that God supplies his needs through the Philippians, and he writes a letter of gratitude. The gifts of the Philippians please God and delights Paul (Phil 4:10-18), and (6) To prove his love for Corinthians, Paul decides to spend everything even himself (2 Cor 12:15). Paul loves Corinthians as if the parents love their children, for children should

Self-Supporting Church

Every Pauline church is financially independent from the beginning. Paul obviously neither receives regular financial help from his converts nor gives to the new believers. He would rather encourage them to help other needy churches in other country.[99] He collects offerings from the believers of Macedonia and Achaia and brings the alms to Jerusalem (11:28-30; 24:17). Paul does this to demonstrate the unity of the church. It does not mean that the Jerusalem church depends upon the churches in other provinces, or that this proceeding lays down a principle of church finance. Paul hopes that this generous gift, given out of deep poverty, would help to close relations between the Jewish and Gentile segments of the Christian church.[100] He does not seem to administer any local church's money himself; he lets every church do their own administration of funds. He does not seem to mention the centralization of church funds or any similar system of controlling church money.[101]

---

not save up for their parents, but parents for their children (Calvinian Theology and Missions [Seoul: Sung Kwang Publishing Co., 1988], 230-32).

[99]Wayne Allen, however, presents some negative points when national church leaders have subsidies from abroad as follows: (1) the initiation of subsidy signals a move away from reliance on lay leadership to reliance on a professional clergy, (2) the paid workers begin to focus more on pleasing the paying agency than on meeting the needs of their churches, and (3) when the local church realizes that their pastor receives foreign subsidy, they lose their sense of ownership of the pastor ("When the Mission Pays the Pastor," *Evangelical Missions Quarterly* 34 [April 1998]: 176-81). William J. Konfield also insists that financial paternalism must be avoided because of the following reasons: (1) it creates dependency, (2) it separates the people who get the money from those who do not, (3) it implies that the church cannot grow, or in some cases even exist, in its own native soil apart from foreign money ("What Hath Our Western Money and Our Western Gospel Wrought?" Evangelical Missions Quarterly 27 [July 1991]: 230-32). Harvie M. Conn criticizes the "self-support myth" for robbing the missionary sending churches and host churches of the joy of mutual giving. He cites biblical data to support his contention that it is the time to end the double standard of funding missions work. He asks, "Has the accepted pattern of missionary support not made it impossible for North American churches to share in the fellowship of receiving as well as giving? Has the accepted pattern of missionary support not made it impossible for North American churches to taste the joyful expression of Christian charity from the world body of Christ? Have we not succeeded in impoverishing ourselves and our brothers in Christ by closing biblical channels for us all to express, through our gifts, the unity of the new man into which Christ has brought us all, the display of Christian love? " ("The Money Barrier Between Sending and Receiving Churches," Evangelical Missions Quarterly 14 [October 1978]: 237-38).

[100]Roland Allen, 52.

[101]In Pauline literatures, there is no mention that Paul gives financial aids to the churches or any leaders of the church. Paul expects them to manage their own affairs and pay their own way even though many of them were extremely poor (2 Cor 8:2). Poverty is no hindrance to progress. They were to live within their means and support the local work, including works of charity. The Galatians are exhorted to support their own teachers (Gal 6:6).

Paul's Strategies in Team Ministry

In Paul's ministry, he does not desire to go his own way or do his own thing. He believes wholeheartedly in teamwork.[102] A tendency to understand Paul as a self-sufficient missionary is not a real portrait of him. Paul seems to have a great capacity for making friendship, and he does this best in association with others.[103] Paul's strategies in team ministry may be noted in terms of its profile and methods.

A Profile of Paul's Team Ministry

Unlike some other early church leaders such as Peter (10:1-48), Stephen (6:7-7:60), and Philip (8:5-14, 26-40) who seem to work alone, Paul launches his ministry as a team member in Antioch church (11:25-26).[104] When the Holy Spirit sets apart Barnabas and Paul for the work to which the Holy Spirit has called and sends them as missionaries to Cyprus, the two missionaries choose one more team member, namely, John (13:5).[105] When Paul could not keep harmony with Barnabas because of the problem of John's sudden return to Jerusalem in the middle of their first missionary journey (13:13), he chooses another co-worker, Silas (15:36-41). In Lystra, Timothy joins Paul's missions team (16:3). Luke, the author of Acts, becomes the fourth member of the team in Troas (16:10).[106] Others in missionary work include Sopater,

---

[102]E. Paimoen, "The Importance of Paul's Missionary Team," *Stulos Theological Journal* 4 (February 1996): 157-73. Paimoen presents various examples of team ministry from Paul's missionary career as documented by Acts and the Pauline letters and implicates Paul's team model for team work for a church development.

[103]There are several evidences that Paul feels aloneness when he is not with other team members. When he comes to Athens and Timothy and Silas are still in Thessalonica, Paul asks people to let the two to join him as soon as possible (Acts 17:15). Paul has no peace of mind when he comes to Troas to preach the gospel of Christ and not meet Titus there (2 Cor 2:12-13), and has fears when he comes to Macedonia (2 Cor 7:5).

[104]The ministry of Barnabas and Paul in Antioch church are so successful that they multiply the number of prophets and teachers who can stand at the same line with Barnabas and Paul in the church one hundred fifty percent; from two to five (Acts 13:1).

[105]I. Howard Marshall argues that John was merely a helper, not in the same group as the prophets and teachers listed in Acts 13:1-3, and not sent by the Holy Spirit. Further, Paul's practice is to take young men with him as his assistants in the work.

He suspects that this particular appointment of taking John as helper is made in good faith. He asserts that John has family links with the island and that this is why he is chosen to accompany the other missionaries (*The Acts of the Apostles: The Tyndale New Testament Commentaries*, [Leicester, England: Inter-Varsity Press, 1983], 218). F. F. Bruce, however, takes the word, 'attendant' or 'helper' to mean a co-worker who can help the team with his special knowledge of certain important phases of the story of Jesus, in particular the passion narrative. Bruce insists that the Greek, ὑπηρετης, rendered 'helper' (Acts 13:5) can be translated as 'minister' comparing with the use of the word in Luke 1:2, ὑπηρεται . . . του λογου, 'ministers of the word' (*The Book of the Acts*, 263).

Aristarchus, Secundus, Gaius, Tychicus, and Trophimus (20:4). Obviously, Paul considers the missions work as a cooperative task, rather than as an individual effort. This is evident in his continuing association with his co-workers and his home church in Antioch.[107]

Methods of Paul's Team Ministry

Paul works always with his missions team and churches.[108] As the leader of his missions team, Paul employs various methods to direct his team. He usually selects local people to work together in missions. Paul and Barnabas choose Cyprus for their first mission field because Barnabas and John are the natives of this region (13:4-5).[109] In Lystra, Paul selects Timothy, a local resident, who has a Greek father and a Jewish mother to his missions team (16:1-3). When the Holy Sprit leads Paul's missions team to Europe, Luke, a physician from Philippi, joins the team (16:10).[110] In Corinth, Aquila and Priscilla, a native of Pontus, joins in Paul's missions team (18:2). When Paul moves to Asia from Corinth, this couple accompanies with Paul and stays in Ephesus that is near their home province (18:18, 24-26).

Paul works with churches and maintains close relationship with them. He normally visits a church after completing his missionary activities (13:1; 14:26-28; 15:4, 40). He learns how to relate to his sending church and other churches that he does not plant directly, including the churches in Jerusalem and Rome (20:17; 21:4, 7,

---

[106]F. F. Bruce, *The Book of the Acts*, 327. William Barclay suggests "Luke met Paul then because Paul needed his professional services, because he was in ill-health which barred him from making the journeys he would like. If this is so it is a great thought to think that Paul took even his weakness and his pain as a messenger from God. It was the sight of a man from Macedonia which finally gave Paul his guidance where to go. Who was this man Paul saw in the vision? Some think it was Luke himself, for Luke may have been a Macedonian" (*The Acts of the Apostles* [Edinburgh, England: The Saint Andrew Press, 1952], 131).

[107]Harold R. Cook notes that missionaries have twofold ministry: ministry to the Gentile and ministry to the home church (*Missionary Life and Work* [Chicago: Moody Press, 1959], 137).

[108]Howard Norrish presents the advantages of a lone ranger and the disadvantages of team member as following: (1) A lone ranger can easily develop a credible self-image or identity among people, but for a team member, it is hard, (2) A lone ranger has the freedom of action and movement, but a team member has to follow the policy, (3) A lone ranger can minimize the possibility of security breaches than a team member of an agency, (4) A lone ranger can minimize the cumbersome administrative works, but a team member has to meet all regulations or rules. The disadvantages of a lone ranger and advantages of a team member are: (1) A lone ranger can easily experience spiritual burnout, but a team member are to be supported by the agency, (2) A lone ranger has no opportunity to be checked objectively by an expert, (3) A lone ranger has lesser opportunity to have orientation or training, a team member has, and (4) A lone ranger may not have many general support like health insurance, pensions, strong prayer supports and others, but a team member has ("Lone Ranger: Yes or No?" *Evangelical Missions Quarterly* 26 [January 1990]: 6-11).

[109]Marshall, 218.

[110]Bruce, *The Book of the Acts*, 308.

8, 17). He welcomes these churches to participate in his missions work.[111]

Paul moves his co-workers around as occasions required (17:15; 18:5; 19:22; 19:5, 14, 17). They would deliver Paul's letter or instructions to the church and bring him news from the churches (18:27; 19:22). In this way, Paul increases his effectiveness as an apostle to the Gentile world. He considers his missions team members not simply as assistants, helpers, or subordinates, but colleagues in ministry.[112]

Paul exercises strong leadership. He executes what he has decided even in the face of opposition from ministry partners. When Paul, for instance, plans to visit Jerusalem, many of his co-workers from places try to persuade him not to enter into Jerusalem as warned by the Holy Spirit. He, however, disregards his co-workers' warning and carries through with his plan (18:20; 21:3, 12-14). Yet, Paul practices his leadership with humility as he takes advices from other leaders. He claims to have served the church with great humility and with tears (20:19) while supplying his needs and that of his companions by his trade, tent-making (18:3; 20:34). Following the suggestion of elders, he pays for the expenses of the purification rites (21:23-26).

Paul's Strategies in Contextualized Communication

Whenever Paul preaches the gospel, he faces cultural differences with the local audience.[113] The cultural gap between the messenger and the recipients usually appears as a major barrier in good communication, and it often causes the recipients to regard

---

[111]Zahn states that when Paul writes a letter to Roman Christians in Corinth,

several house-church congregations have existed already in Rome. Paul's first concern in writing to Rome is to establish a connection between him and the Roman church, and thus, Paul intends to involve the Roman church in his mission to Spain that represents the
uttermost part of the earth (Rom. 15:24, 28-32), (T. Zahn, *Introduction to the New Testament*, vol. 1, trans. J. M. Trout [Grand Rapids, MI: Kregel Publications, 1953], 352).

[112]W. H. Ollrog asserts that "three categories of associates are distinguished among Paul's missions team: First, the most intimate circle, comprising Barnabas, Silas, and particularly Timothy; second, the 'the independent co-workers,' such as Priscilla and Aquila, and Titus; and third, and perhaps most important, representatives from local churches, such as Epaphroditus, Epaphras, Aristarchus, Gaius, and Jason. The churches put these persons at Paul's disposal for limited periods. Through them the churches themselves are represented in the Pauline mission and become co-responsible for the work. As a matter of fact, not being represented in this venture constitutes a shortcoming in a local church; such a church has excluded itself from participating in the Pauline missionary enterprise" ("Paulus und seine Mitarbeiter" [Neukirchen-Vluyn: Neukirchener Verlag, 1979], 92-122; quoted in David J. Bosch, *Transforming Mission: Paradigm Shifts in Theology of Mission* [Maryknoll, NY: Orbis Books, 1991], 132).

[113]R. Daniel Shaw, "Cultural and Evangelism: A Moder for Missiological Strategy," *Missiology* 18 (July 1990): 291-304.

the gospel as a religious and cultural intruder or demolisher.[114] Various efforts, thus, on how to make the gospel more understandable and relevant to the target culture has been sought.[115] Paul comprehends these aspects fully and invests a significant effort for effective gospel transplant. The following pages, therefore, will show how Paul contextualizes local customs and the gospel message.[116]

Contextualizing Local Customs

Since Christianity originates from Judaism, and Paul himself is a Jew, he cannot amputate completely the influences of Judaic culture from his ministries.[117] The other factor that he faces is Hellenism that dominates the Roman Empire. Paul, thus, strives to desert Christianity from both worlds and to make it universal. Paul's efforts of contextualizing local customs may be noted in terms of (1) the issue of circumcision, (2) the issue of rituals, and (3) the issue of one gospel.

The Issue of Circumcision

The main theme disputed in the Jerusalem Council is whether circumcision is the

---

[114]David J. Hesselgrave and Edward Rommen, *Contextualization: Meanings, Methods, and Models* (Grand Rapids, MI: Baker Book House, 1989), 11.

[115]David Racey stimulates the narrow definition of contextualization must be developed relevantly by many Christian cross-cultural workers according to their own setting ("Contextualization: How Far is Too Far?" *Evangelical Missions Quarterly* 32, [July 1996], 305). Paul G. Hiebert emphasizes the importance of anthropology in missionary works. He presents five points how anthropology can help the missions: (1) It can bring understanding of cross-cultural situations, (2) It can provide us with many insights into such specific mission tasks as Bible translation, (3) It can help missionaries understand the processes of conversion, (4) It can help us make the gospel relevant to our listeners and (5) It can help us relate to people around the world in all their cultural diversity and assist us in building bridges of understanding between them (*Anthropological Insights for Missionaries* [Grand Rapids, MI: Baker Book House, 1985], 15-16).

[116]Daniel Sanchez asserts that Paul contextualized the message by taking into account the socio-cultural and religious background of his hearers ("Contextualization and the Missionary Endeavor," in *Missiology: An Introduction to the Foundations, History, and Strategies of World Missions*, ed. John Mark Terry, Ebbie Smith and Justice Anderson [Nashville, Tennessee: Broadman and Holman Publishers, 1998], 319). Byung-Kwan Jung emphasizes the "missionary sociology" in the study of missions. He writes that the interaction between a society and its individuals influences missions, on the other side, missions influences the society and its individuals (*The Challenges to the Modern Ministry and Missions* [Seoul: The Word of Life Press, 1994],11-16).

[117]John M. G. Barclay asserts, "Paul emerges as one quite highly assimilated, but comparatively low in accumulation and accommodation. Anomalously, Paul deracinates a culturally conservative form of Judaism for the sake of his largely Gentile churches. Paul was consistently repudiated as a apostate, despite his continuing loyalties to the Jewish people" ("Paul Among Diaspora Jews: Anomaly or Apostate?" *Journal for the Study of the New Testament* 60, [December 1995]: 89-120). See also D. J. Harrington, "Paul and Judaism: 5 Puzzles," *Bible Review* 9 (February 1993): 18-25, 52.

condition of salvation (15:5-6). The resolution of the Council is that the Gentile Christians do not need to be circumcised or to keep the Mosaic Law to be authentic Christians (15:10). The Council discusses one more issue presented by the Antioch Church thus: What are the conditions for table fellowship between Jewish Christians and Gentile Christians?[118] The resolution to the second issue states, "You are to abstain from food sacrificed to idols, from blood, from the meat of strangled animals, and from sexual immorality" (15:29).[119] By the decision of the council, the Gentile Christians acquire equal status and may have full fellowship with Jewish Christians. The Council removes the cultural partitioning wall between the two.[120] The results of the Jerusalem Council, thus, stimulate Paul more to expedite contextualized messages and theologies for Gentile converts.

The resolution of Jerusalem Council clears Paul's position on circumcision, not to circumcise the new Gentile believers.[121] Paul, however, circumcises Timothy after the Jerusalem Council (16:3). On the other hand, he lets Titus not to be circumcised.[122] The two cases show that he is not an obstinate and inconsistent person. Paul circumcises Timothy because he is a Jew by Jewish law that counts a man Jew if his mother is Jewish (16:1). Because of his un-circumcision, Timothy appears technically an apostate Jew. The third reason to circumcise Timothy may be a practical purpose that is, his greater usefulness in the ministry of the gospel among the Jews.[123] Titus is non-

---

[118]F. F. Bruce explains the background why the second agenda becomes the naturally following issue in the council, thus: "Centuries of devotion to the laws governing food and purity had bred in [many Jewish Christians] an instinctive revulsion from eating with Gentiles which could not be immediately overcome. Gentiles quite happily ate certain kinds of food, which Jews had been taught to abominate, and the laxity of Gentile morals, especially where relations between the sexes were concerned, made the idea of reciprocal hospitality between them and Jewish Christians distasteful" (*New Testament History* [Garden City, NY: Doubleday & Co., Inc., 1971], 286).

[119]H. R. Johne, "The Prohibitions in the Jerusalem Council's Letter to Gentile Believers," *Wisconsin Lutheran Quarterly* 94 (January 1997): 47-48. Johne asserts that when Christian love requires abstention from an αδιαφορον, that the prohibition is a binding as the Ten Commandments are.

[120]Norman R. Ericson, "Implications from the New Testament for Testament Contextualization," in *Thoelogy and Mission*, ed. David J. Hesselgrave (Grand Rapids, MI: Baker Book House, 1978), 75.

[121]Paul is a strong advocate of anti-circumcision. For Paul, the only thing that counts is faith expressing itself through love (Gal 5:6). In Romans, Paul writes, "A man is not a Jew if he is only one outwardly, nor is circumcision merely outward and physical. No, a man is a Jew if he is one inwardly, and circumcision is circumcision of the heart, by the Spirit, not by the written code. Such a man's praise is not from men, but from God" (Rom 2:28-29).

[122]Gal 2:3.

[123]F.F. Bruce, *The Book of the Acts*, rev. ed. (Grand Rapids, MI: WM. B. Eerdmans Publishing Co., 1988), 304. J. Herbert Kane elaborates on the question of Paul's appearing inconsistency as follows: "The answer is: the good of the work. Paul knew that not everyone shared his lofty views regarding circumcision; therefore he would gladly go along with them in their ignorance or prejudice. He was prepared to fight the world, the flesh, and the devil; but he refused to fight his brothers in Christ over matters which, to him at least, were not a fundamental part of the gospel. . . . Paul's understanding of the gospel in Galatians Chapter one should not be divorced from his attitude toward the gospel preachers in

Jew so that he does not need to be circumcised.

The Issue of Rituals

Though Paul's world in the first century is under the Roman political power, Hellenism dominates the Empire in cultural aspect. Unlike the Judaists who are monotheists, Hellenistic Gentiles are polytheists or pantheists and idol-worshippers. Paul accepts the resolution of the Jerusalem Council that requires the Gentile Christians to avoid food sacrificed to idols, blood, the meat of strangled animals, and sexual immorality corresponding to the laws in Old Testament. The Council requests these four prohibitions as minimum of ritual cleanness. In his second missions journey, Paul delivers the decision of Jerusalem Council to the believers and requires them to observe it (16:5).[124] Because of these requirements, the owner of the fortune-telling slave girl and the magistrates in Philippi rationalize to strip and beat Paul and Silas (16:21-22). Paul feels free from eating anything because he believes that everything on earth is the Lord's, and, accordingly he eats in the jailor's house (16:34). But when his freedom causes problems to others, he would refuse to eat.[125] Likewise, Paul's primary attitude toward anything nonessential of the gospel is flexible.

The Issue of One Gospel

For Paul, idolatry is one of the most decisive violations of the gospel so that he leaves no space for compromising with it. Paul's concept of one God is found clearly in his sermons (13:26-41; 14:15-17; 16:31; 17:23-31; 25:19; 26:23). His sole message is turning to God in repentance and has faith in Jesus Christ, the Lord (20:21). He rejects other gospel which is tainted by Judaism or others, because it is anti-gospel and it pleases human beings instead of pleasing God. Paul strives to keep the purity of the gospel. When the legalists, for instance, defile the gospel in Antioch church, he argues desperately against those from Judea (15:1-2). Though Hellenistic religions also retain virtues similar with the gospel and Paul himself was raised in the Hellenistic religion

---

Philippians chapter one" (*Christian Missions in Biblical Perspective, 85*). Ronald Y. K Fung notes that if Titus was circumcised in Jerusalem, the fact would be well advertised in Galatia by Paul's opponents who attempted to make an atmosphere to compel Titus to be circumcised. Paul avoided that Titus was a test case because some legalistic false brothers were spying on them (*The Epistle to the Galatians: The New International Commentary on the New Testament* [Grand Rapids, MI: William B. Eerdmans Publishing Company, 1989], 91).

[124] See Num 25:1-4; Dan 1:8; Lev 3:17; Deut 12:16, 23, 25, 27; Isa 65:4; Ezek 4:14. The main problem that calls the Jerusalem council was actually circumcision, but the resolution statement of the meeting contains not the main issue. However, the fact that it is not included among the necessary things for Gentile converts to observe means that the demand for its observance (Acts 15:1,5) was disallowed (F.F. Bruce, *The Acts of the Apostles: Greek Text with Introduction and Commentary* [Grand Rapids, MI: William B. Eerdmans Publishing Company, 1990], 347).

[125] 1 Cor 10:25-30.

dominating society,[126] he rejects the idolatry and introduces a new positive attitude, namely, "agape."[127]

Contextualizing Gospel Message

Paul mobilizes all possible contextualized methods to transplant the gospel in the Gentile world. Paul's efforts of contextualizing the gospel message may be noted in terms of using local languages and local symbols.

The Use of Local Language

On the Day of Pentecost, when people hear the wonders of God in their own language emphasizes the importance of the local language for the advancement of the gospel. If people do not hear the gospel in their local tongue, they are not only limited in their own understanding, but also they are limited to relate the message to others. The new believers expect to receive the gospel and be trained in their local language.[128] Speaking the local language is of primary importance in Paul's ministry. He employs different languages, in different places, and in different situations. During his arrest, for instance, in Jerusalem temple, Paul requests from the commander a chance to address the people in Greek. Astonished by Paul's fluent Greek, the commander permits him to speak to the people. This time he replaces Greek with Aramaic to get the attention of people who are rushing to kill him. When the fiery mob hear him speaks to them in their vernacular language, they immediately become quiet. This provides him opportunity to deliver his message more effectively (Acts 21:37-22:2). Paul as a rabbi learned under Gamaliel, seems to know Hebrew, the Old Testament language also (22:3). Beside Hebrew, he seems to understand the Lycaonian language (14:11-12) and Latin, the language of politics and military in Roman Empire. This is because he plans to preach the gospel in Rome (19:21) and Spain, known then as the end of the earth.[129]

---

[126] Walther von Loewenich, *Paul: His Life and Work* (London: Oliver and Boyd, 1960), 13.

[127] Daniel Patte, *Paul's Faith and the Power of the Gospel: A Structural Introduction to the Pauline Letters* (Philadelphia, PA: Fortress Press, 1983), 69-70.

[128] Charles Brock, *The Principles and Practice of Indigenous Church Planting* (Nashville, TN: Broadman Press, 1981), 39-40. Lyman E. Reed agrees with Brock and stresses the importance of language, thus: "One of the key areas in preparing missionaries for intercultural communication is the need for adequate language learning. Language is an integral aspect of culture. Since it is the vehicle of communication among people, it is especially important for missionaries to know the language (Preparing Missionaries for Intercultural Communication: A Bi-cultural Approach [Pasadena, CA: William Carey Library, 1985], 59). E. Thomas Brewster and Elizabeth S Brewster, "What It Takes to Learn a Language and Get Involved with People," Evangelical Missions Quarterly 14 (April 1978): 101-5. See also Carol V. McKinney, "Which Language: Trade or Minority? " Missiology 18 (July 1990): 289.

[129] See Rom 15:34. See also J. Blauw, *The Missionary Nature of the Church* (New York: McGraw-Hill, 1962), 103.

The Use of Local Symbols

Paul begins his messages from the place where his hearers are; otherwise the message will be foreign to the audience. If the message appears foreign to the audience, it would work as a good excuse to reject the message. Paul, therefore, strives to make his message understandable to all people in all cultures by using local symbols.[130] His contextualized messages are observable in terms of messages for the monotheists, the polytheists, and the pantheistically inclined Athenian philosophers

Message for the Monotheists

Paul's audiences in the synagogues are Jews and Gentile God-fearers who have pre-knowledge about the Old Testament. He, thus, precedes his message from their symbol, the history of Hebrew nation. In Damascus synagogue, his very first message after his conversion is that "Jesus is the Son of God" (9:20), the equivalent to "the Messiah," in keeping with Psalm 2:7.[131] Paul's message resonates the theme of the Gospel of Matthew that aims for the Jews. As the main audience in Pisidian Antioch synagogue, Paul opens his preaching with "The God of the people of Israel chose our fathers" (13:17). The fact that God chooses Israel as His covenant people is one of the outstanding emphases of the Old Testament (Exod 6:1,4,6; Deut 7:6-8), and Paul uses this symbol discreetly in his preaching for the monotheists, the Jews.

Message for the Polytheists

In Lystra, Paul's hearers are purely polytheists who possess different symbols from the monotheists. He approaches them by performing a miracle, healing a lame from his mother's womb (14:8-10). It captivates a great attention of the local people and an unpredictable opportunity for the advance of the gospel. To the priest of Zeus and the people who try to offer sacrifices to Paul and Barnabas, Paul preaches the gospel emphasizing the fact that the one who heals the lame man is not them, but God (14:15-17). He then makes an appeal to the natural revelation of God, the Creator in the forefront.[132] Paul casts out a spirit from a slave girl fortuneteller in Philippi. Although Paul and Silas are flogged and thrown into prison because of this power conflict, it caused great advance of Christianity in Philippi (16:16-21).

---

[130]Hesselgrave, *Planting Churches Cross-Culturally,* 207-8.

[131] Charles W. Carter and Ralph Earle, *The Acts of the Apostles* (Grand Rapids, MI: Zondervan Publishing House, 1978), 130.

[132]Bruce, *The Book of the Acts,* 292.

Message for the Pantheists

To the pantheistically inclined Athenian philosophers, Paul begins his messages by using the local symbols like an altar of "unknown God," a Greek poem, and images (17:23, 28, 29).[133] He penetrates the mind of his audiences, Epicurean and Stoic philosophers, and presents gospel relevant in their context. In his message, Paul answers three great questions of the philosophy: whence-the origin of all things, what-the nature of all things, and wither-the end of all things (17:24-32).[134] These three questions are never answered to those philosophers. Paul's presentation of a personal, supreme, and transcendent God who created all things by a divine fiat is an answer to the question of origin, for which philosophers has long sought in vain. Paul does not argue with local people on a different worldview. He enters into local people's frame of reference and advocates the gospel effectively.[135]

Summary of the Chapter

In this chapter, the researcher investigates Paul's six missions strategies found in Acts 13-28. The first one investigated is Paul's church planting strategy. Paul chooses cities for the location of planting churches with several reasons. He also chooses receptive people as primary target. If the receptivity is low in one place, he moves immediately to other place. Paul's effective methods for church planting including house churches, household conversion, personal evangelism, evangelism in public, shorter stay in one place, and role modeling in the church were discussed.

The second strategy investigated was Paul's preaching strategy. This included the content of his message, the attitude he takes towards other religions, and the methods he employs in dealing with other religion. The character of Paul's preaching, including clearness, persuasiveness, urgency, Scripture-orientation, and contextualization were also investigated.

The third strategy investigated deals with ways Paul equips church leaders. Noted were the status of Pauline church leadership, divine guidance, synagogue tradition, and women leadership. Proven people and local leadership are the two qualifications of

---

[133] Hesselgrave, *Planting Churches Cross-Culturally*, 208.

[134] Jun-Seop Kim, *An Introduction to Philosophy* (Seoul: Bak Young Sa, 1977), 261-62. See also Carter and Earle, *The Acts of the Apostles*, 259-63. See also N. C. Croy, "Hellenistic Philosophies and the Preaching of the Resurrection (Acts 17:18,32)," *Novum Testamentum* 39 (January 1997): 21-39.

[135] Charles H. Kraft states, "Effective communication starts with an attempt on the part of the communicator to relate identificationally with the audience and succeeds best when they are able to relate reciprocally to both messenger and message" (*Christianity in Culture: A Study in Dynamic Biblical Theologizing in Cross-Cultural Perspective* [Maryknoll, NY: Orbis Books, 1979], 162).

leadership in Pauline churches. For the foundation of Paul's equipping ministry, doctrinal, practical, and spiritual foundations are noted. The methods that Paul employed for equipping ministry included regular teaching, formal institution, and reinforcement.

The fourth strategy researched was the financial matter. Paul's self-supporting principle applicable for both missionaries and churches in Pauline ministries was discussed respectively.

The fifth strategy investigated was Paul's team ministry. The profile of his team ministry explored who, where, why, and how of the team. The method of his team ministry investigated how he operates his team effectively. This section discussed also how Paul maintained good relationship with home church, how he contacted the remote churches, and how he exercised his leadership among the team members.

The sixth strategy searched was how Paul presents the gospel relevantly and appropriately in various cultural settings, contextualizaed communication. This section explored how he deals with the Judaic custom prudently and Hellenistic culture wisely. His hearers were monotheistic Diaspora Jews, polytheistic Greeks, and pantheistic philosophers.

Chapter Two

MISSIONS STRATEGIES OF THE KOREAN PRESBYTERIAN MISSIONARIES IN CENTRAL AND SOUTHERN PHILIPPINES

Churches in the Philippines have grown rapidly, especially during the last two decades.[136] In parallel with the national movement of church growth, the Presbyterian Church of the Philippines has grown in quantity especially in central and southern Philippines during the 1990s. Korean Presbyterian missionaries in central and southern Philippines appear to contribute significantly to the national effort of evangelization. The number of Presbyterian Church of the Philippines increased from 37 in 1990 to 164 in 2000. In central and southern Philippines, the number of Presbyterian churches grew from 5 in 1990 to 64 in 2000, and the number of baptized members increased from 50 to 1,660 in the same period.[137] This indicates 1,280% growth in the number of churches and a 3,320 % growth in the number of baptized believers during the last ten years. Thus, discovering what missions strategies the Korean Presbyterian missionaries in central and southern Philippines have employed is a significant step in understanding some relevant and appropriate ways to evangelize the nation.

There are four different missions groups of the Korean Presbyterian Church with thirty-one missionaries assigned to central and southern Philippines.[138] The main

---

[136] The Filipino church's Average Annual Growth Rate between 1985 and 1990 is 5.1%. Protestant church members are 7.5% of the total population of the nation. See Patrick Johnstone, *Operation World*, 5th ed. (Carlisle, UK: OM Publishing, 1993: reprint, with corrections, Carlisle, UK: OM Publishing, 1995), 16, 448.

[137] Presbyterian Church of the Philippines, *PILIPINAS* (n.p., 1990), n.p. "Directory of Churches" (Souvenir Program, 5th General Assembly of the Presbyterian Church of the Philippines, Dasmarinas City, Cavite, October 17-18, 2000), 13-21. Edmund Matulac, "Annual Statistical Report" Souvenir Program, The 9th Stated Meeting of the Visayas Presbytery, Davao City, December 5-6, 2000), n.p.

[138] See Footnote 4 in the Introduction.

missions stations are in Cebu City, Iloilo City, Dumaguete City, and Davao City. In conducting the research, thirty-one sets of questionnaires were sent to and collected from the missionaries who are working with the Visayas Presbytery of the PCP. All thirty-one missionaries responded to the survey questionnaire.

This chapter analyzes and presents the missions strategies of the Korean Presbyterian missionaries in central and southern Philippines based on the completed questionnaires. There are two parts in this chapter. The first part presents basic information about Korean Presbyterian missionaries and their work in central and southern Philippines, and the second part deals with their missions strategies.

Basic Information about the Korean Presbyterian Missionaries and Work in Central and Southern Philippines

Information gathered regarding status and the historical background of the work of the PCP in central and southern Philippines may help in understanding the missions strategies employed by Korean Presbyterian missionaries in this region. This section, thus, lays out the basic information about Korean Presbyterian missionaries in central and southern Philippines as follows: (1) A brief history and missions work of the four missions groups of the Korean Presbyterian Church, and (2) An analysis of the general information of the missionaries.

A Brief History and Work of the Four Missions Groups of the Korean Presbyterian Church

Four Korean Presbyterian missions groups work in central and southern Philippines with PCP are KPCK, KPCH, KPCT, and KPCKH. This section, thus, reveals briefly the history and work of these four missions groups respectively.

A Brief History and Work of the KPCK

The first KPCK missionary in central and southern Philippines was Rev. Hoo-Soo Nam and his family.[139] The Foreign Missions Board of the KPCK commissioned the

---

[139]This section on the history and work of the KPCK is reconstructed mainly from the researcher's personal diary, reports of work presented to the Foreign Missions Board of KPCK, personal prayer letters, the minutes of KPCK missionary meetings, brochures and journals of PCP, and other fellow missionaries' reports and prayer letters. The researcher interviewed some co-missionaries and exchanged letters with

Nams for missionary service at the Ulsan Presbyterian Church, Ulsan City, Korea, on August 26, 1987. The Nams arrived in the Philippines on September 4, 1987 and began to plant new churches after two years of their language training. Nam started the Visayas Mission Church (VMC) with Korean members on the last Sunday of September, 1987, and has since engaged in planting other churches and theological education.

Rev. Hyung-Kyu Kim and his family were commissioned with the Nams together, but arrived in the Philippines on December 7, 1987. After the arrival of the Kims, Nam and Kim agree to serve the VMC for two months alternately until the church called a full-time pastor. Under the leadership of Nam and Kim, the VMC grew rapidly and started to help the Port Christian Center in a slum in Cebu City on May 8, 1989. Both missionaries also participated in many other missions related work afterward. Nam and Kim handed over the Korean church to Rev. Byung-Man An on July 8, 1990 and concentrated on their primary missions for the local people.

Following the policy of the Foreign Missions Board of KPCK, to work with the existing Reformed Presbyterian Church in each missions field, Nam and Kim joined the PCP as regular members on March 23, 1988.[140] All succeeding missionaries after them joined the PCP. Kim was elected as the moderator of GPPCP on October 9, 1991, whileNam was elected first moderator of the Visayas Presbytery on June 5, 1996, and the second moderator of the GAPCP on October 21, 1997.[141]

On May 1989, Sung-Il Kim and his family arrived to Cebu City as commissioned by the Kimhae Presbytery of KPCK and moved to Dumaguete City to pursue his higher theological education, a requirement for his ordination and missionary work. He completed his master of divinity degree at the Divinity School of Silliman University, in Dumaguete City. After one year additional study in Korea Theological Seminary, he was ordained and appointed as a regular missionary by the Foreign Missions Board of KPCK. He planted churches in Dumaguete City and Negros Oriental.

On August 29, 1989, Nam and Kim made a five-year-plan and sent it to the

---

those who were out of country to collect more accurate information and resources.

[140] One year before the KPCK missionaries came to the Philippines, the executive secretary and other members of KPCK Foreign Missions Board made three articles of agreement with KPCH missionaries in Manila on August 16, 1986. One of the three articles is to organize one Presbyterian Church in the Philippines together. However, KPCH missionaries organized PCP a few months before the arrival of KPCK missionaries. KPCK missionaries respect the agreement and joined the PCP.

[141] The Office of the General Secretary of the General Presbytery of the Presbyterian Church of the Philippines, "*The Minutes of the General Presbytery of the Presbyterian Church of the Philippines (From Inaugural Session to 19th Assembly: June 27, 1987 – October 5,6, 1994)*" (Quezon City, Philippines: n.p.,1995), 34. From 1987 to 1996, the official name of PCP is The General Presbytery of the Presbyterian Church of the Philippines (GPPCP). When the church grew in number and size, GPPCP divided its organization into three Presbyteries and organized the General Assembly of the Presbyterian Church of the Philippines (GAPCP).

Foreign Missions Board of KPCK for approval. The plan aims to build a multi-purpose missions center on 100,000 m^2 area, which includes a theological seminary, dormitory, medical clinic, kindergarten, elementary school, high school, missionary training center, and a guest house. The plan attempts to invite fifty missionaries to operate the multi-purpose missions center. However, the Foreign Mission Board of KPCK deferred the approval of such plan due to other crucial matters at that time. The missions project was taken up again in June 1991 and June 1996 by the KPCK missionaries in the Philippines.

On October 17, 1989, Miss Young-Sook Kim, a missionary nurse arrived in the Philippines and began to work in Silliman University medical center in Dumaguete City. After working at the said hospital for one and a half year, she moved to Danao City, Cebu where she started a day-care center in cooperation with Danao Presbyterian Church in April 1991. Kim completed her missionary work on October 1992 and returned to Korea.

The year 1990 was a turning point for the missions of KPCK in central and southern Philippines. The KPCK missionaries launched its first theological education ministry by introducing reformed theology to Presbyterian leaders and pastors of other denominations. On January 16-26, 1990, with the help of Presbyterian Theological Seminary (PTS) in Dasmariñas, Cavite, Rev. Cornellius Castillo conducted seminars on Pastoral Counseling for the first week, and Rev. Gerardo Kim, president of PTS then, taught Presbyterianism the week after. Gerardo Kim, in fact, first introduced the idea to open a PTS extension program in Cebu. The idea was accepted, developed, and implemented later by Rev. Hyung Kyu Kim and Rev. Hoo-Soo Nam. Hyung-Kyu Kim became the director of PTS extension in Cebu, while Nam was in charge of administrative work. This Cebu extension classes operated until 1995. When Nam constructed a multipurpose missions center in Mandaue City in 1995, the PTS extension program was incorporated into the educational ministry of the Cebu Bible College. In June 1995, Hyung-Kyu Kim became the first President of Cebu Bible College, Nam was appointed the Academic Dean, and Ki-Hong Kim as the Dean of Student Affairs. However, Hyung-Kyu relocated to Korea on April 17, 1996, and Ki-Hong returned to Korea for further studies in May 1996.[142] Nam continued the position of President and Academic Dean together, working with Rev. Edmund Matulac as Dean of Student Affairs, Mrs. Eulesa Matulac as Registrar, and Mrs. Sung-Hee Nam Lee as Business Manager.

By 1990, the KPCK planted five churches on the islands of Cebu and Mindanao. On February 4, 1990, Nam started the Bogo Presbyterian Church (BPC) in Bogo, Cebu, 100 kilometers away from Cebu City. Nam received permission to use one of the classrooms of Cebu Roosevelt Memorial College for Sunday worship from Dr. Eliot Lepiten, the President. Nam turned the ministry over to Rev. E. Azarcon on May 1990.

---

[142]Ki-Hong Kim joins with the Cebu Bible College in March 1995. Although he is not a member missionary of KPCK, he joins the school individually on an individual basis.

On February 18, 1990, the KPCK planted the Mandaue Presbyterian Church (MPC) in Mandaue City, Cebu. The first worker for the church was Mr. Elvin Celerio who was then a student of PTS and was serving as a ministry intern. Under the leadership of Rev. Edmund Matulac, the church became a self-supporting church.

On April 8, 1990, the KPCK started Danao Presbyterian Church (DPC). Rev. Manuel Maca served as the pastor of the church from the beginning. The church developed a feeding program for children from poor families, that became the basis of its holistic ministry. This program grew gradually and became an elementary school.

On June 14, 1990, Rev. Hyung-Kyu Kim relocated to Cagayan de Oro City, Mindanao and planted Oro Presbyterian Church (OPC) with the help of pastor Marvin Abello and Iligan Presbyterian Church (IPC), Iligan City, Lanao del Norte with pastor Henrieto Pacaldo. However, Kim transferred to Dasmariñas City, Cavite for teaching at PTS on May 31, 1991.[143] Alongside of Kim's departure for PTS, Rev. Noel Najarro, pastor of OPC, became ill. This situation left the OPC to fold up. However, on July 18, 1993, Nam and Najarro planted the Butuan Presbyterian Church (BPC) utilizing the remaining equipment of OPC in Butuan City, Agusan del Norte, Mindanao.

On July 8, 1990, the KPCK organized Cebu Presbyterian Church (CPC) with the Filipino congregation separated from Korean members of the VMC. The pastor of the church was Rev. Magno Villar. However, this church split into two, CPC and CCC (Cebu Christian Church) due to some issues.

Missionaries of KPCK and national pastors organized themselves on March 5, 1990 and registered it with the Securities and Exchange Commission on December 19, 1990. The members of the group called themselves as the Presbyterian Missions of the Philippine Inc. (PMPI).[144] The incorporators were Hyung-Kyu Kim, Hoo-Soo Nam, Magno Villar, Marvin Abello, Elvin Ceserio, Manuel Maca, Ja-Sun Kim, Calvin Adlawan, and Henrieto Pacaldo. Magno Villar served as the founding chairman of PMPI.

On November 8, 1990, Rev. Jae-Yong Kim and family arrived in the Philippines. After studying the language for five months in Cebu City, the Kims moved to Iloilo City on April 10, 1991, following the PMPI plan to dispose missionaries in every major city in central and southern Philippines.[145] Kim planted churches and opened the Hosanna Bible School in Iloilo City.

---

[143] Carlos Alfredo, telephone interview by researcher, March 12, 2001. Alfredo was the Academic Dean of PTS when he was interviewed.

[144] The initial PMPI will be used hereafter.

[145] Jae-Yong Kim and Young-Sook Yoon, *The Missionary Work in the Philippines: God's Merciful Hands* (Pusan, Korea: Korea Publishing Company, 1995), 29-31.

As part of the holistic missions, Nam started the Presbyterian Vocational Institute (PVI) in Cebu Presbyterian Church on March 26, 1991, with two sewing machines. The trainees were recruited from churches and taught the basic sewing skills in two months. Phil-Sun Sung, a designer and expert in sewing from Inchon, Korea taught the trainees. After one month of training, one local stuff toy company loaned twenty-four industrial sewing machines and other raw materials necessary for stabilizing the supply of workers. The vocational teaching program then became effective tool for evangelism. Many of the trainees attended the church worship and their tithes and offerings helped finance church ministries. The vocational institution stopped after few months when the Nams went on furlough on September 1, 1991.

On May 25, 1991, three new missionary families arrived in the Philippines, namely Rev. Kwang-Suk Choi, Rev. Kyung-Geun Lee, and Rev. Soon-Seong Jeong. The KPCK assigned Choi to Danao Presbyterian Church, Lee to Mandaue Presbyterian Church, and Jeong to Cebu Presbyterian Church. Later, Lee moved to Manila and Jeong relocated to Bacolod City to start new ministries. Choi took over the ministries in Cebu Presbyterian Church and later assisted in theological education ministry.

On May 19, 1992, Jeong-Hee Rho, a missionary nurse, arrived in Cebu City to work with Young-Sook Kim together in Danao Presbyterian Church Day Care Center. When Young-Sook returned to Korea on October, 1992, Rho converted the Day Care Center into the Hosanna Kindergarten School. The Hosanna Kindergarten School grew to become an elementary school, in a matter of two years. While directing the school, Rho joined the Luke Ministry catering the medical needs of members.[146]

Rev. Sung-Gon Hwang and family arrived on June 8, 1994 in the Philippines as a result of a prearranged ministry by Rev. Jae-Yong Kim in Iloilo City under KPCK. Hwang started a student ministry in Iloilo City and assisted the rural development ministry in Bingawan, Iloilo until1998. After resuming ministries from furlough, Hwang transfered to Manila and assisted the theological educational ministry of the Presbyterian Theological Seminary, Dasmariñas, Cavite.[147]

On September 23, 1998, Rev Sung-Joo Shin and family arrived in Cebu City to join the growing faculty of the Cebu Bible College. Shin served as Academic Dean of CBC for a year. He, however, resigned from the College on October 31, 1999.

A Brief History and Work of the KPCH

KPCH was the first Korean Presbyterian group that started to dispatch missionaries to the Philippines in 1977.[148] Rev. Byung-Soo Baik of KPCH was the first

---

[146] Jeong-Hee Rho, telephone interview by researcher, February 26, 2001.

[147] Sung-Gon Hwang, telephone interview by researcher, March 1, 2001.

[148] This section is reconstructed based on the "Brief History of the Mindanao Branch of the

Korean Presbyterian missionary to work in central and southern Philippines. Baik and family moved to Davao city, Mindanao in March 1981 to plant church. He stayed in Davao around one year, then transferred to Manila in 1982, where he supervised the churches. After the Baiks left for furlough, the churches in Davao City struggled to exist and were eventually closed down by EPM in 1990. Baik changed his missions field after furlough and decided not to return to Davao City.

Kyung-Ae Kim arrived in Davao city as a lay single woman missionary in 1989, and started the Bethel Presbyterian Church and Bethel Kindergarten School in the church for evangelism purpose. EPM appointed Rev. Jin-Phil Hur and family to work in Davao City following the agreement of the Manila Decision.[149] On August 12, 1991, Hur moved his family to Davao City and planted Hosanna Presbyterian Church. He also started a Bible school in 1994 which became the Presbyterian Bible College (PBC).[150]

Next to Hur was Rev. Sung-Joon Lee who arrived in Davao City on November 20, 1994. Lee took over all the ministries which Hur handled as the former left for furlough in June 1995. Lee planted the Church of Love and two other churches in Davao city and vicinity, plus a Muslim ministry in Maguindanao tribe in Midsayap, Cotabato since January 2000.

In November 1995, Rev. Seok-Jin Kim and his family joined the KPCH missionaries in Davao City. Kim helped Hur by teaching at the Presbyterian Bible College from June 1997 to December 2000 when he left for furlough and planted two Churches: one in Davao City and one in General Santos City in southern Mindanao area. Kim, especially, started a computer school to evangelize young generation in the area of the New Bataan tribe in May 1998.

Rev. Cheol-Young Jun arrived in Davao City in May 1997. Missionaries of the KPCH in Davao assigned Jun in General Santos city, southern Mindanao where he worked with the Bilaan tribe in General Santos city. Jun opened a center for the eradication of illiteracy and offered Bible classes from October 1998 to December

---

Evangelical Presbyterian Missions (Hereafter referred to as EPM)" prepared by KPCH missionaries in Davao city.

[149]"The Manila Decision" was a result of the Korean Presbyterian missionaries meeting held in PTS, Cavite on April 12, 1991. Around twenty missionaries from four different groups attended and discussed how they could work cooperatively. The main points of Manila Decision were as follows: (1) To organize and to nourish one Filipino Presbyterian Church, (2) To divide missions field; northern Luzon-KPCH, KPCT, KPCC (Korean Presbyterian Church - Conservative), Visayas-KPCK, and Mindanao-KPCK, KPCH; (3) To open one office for PCP in Manila; (4) To operate one seminary; and (5) To operate one missionary training institute. Three representatives appointed by each respective group signed "The Decision." The three representatives were Rev. Hwal-Young Kim of KPCH, Rev. Dong-Won Ryu of KPCT, and Rev. Hyung-Kyu Kim of KPCK. Around 64 missionaries joined the Manila Decision in implementing it.

[150]Jin-Phil Hur, telephone interview by researcher, March 1, 2001.

2000. He also constructed a mission home in General Santos city in April 1999.

The World Missions Board of KPCH requested its missionaries in Davao area to reorganize their ministries into a one-team ministry in February 1999. Thus, KPCH missionaries in southern Mindanao reshaped their organization from individual ministries to a full-scale team ministry in April 1999. KPCH missionaries in Davao area received permission to organize an independent organization, the Mindanao Evangelical Presbyterian Missions (MEPM), from their national body, EPM on February 1, 2000.

Rev. Sang-Sung Kim and his family joined with the MEPM on November 17, 2000. Rev. Sung-Ho Jung and family arrived in Davao City to serve in theological education since March 2000. Rev. In-Sung Son who originally worked in Luzon got the nod from EPM to change his mission field from Lipa City, Batangas to Davao City in February 2000 and then moved to Davao City in April 2000. He was soon followed by Rev. Suck-Tae Lee who was accepted as an associate missionary member of MEPM in April 1999. Lee started his ministry in Iligan City, Lanao del Norte, Mindanao.

Another EPM missionary, although worked in Dumaguete City, Negros Oriental, is Rev. Young-Ku Jee. Jee moved to Dumaguete City from Baguio City on April 8, 1989 and planted churches in Dumaguete City and in neighboring towns. He then established the Dumaguete Bible College in Dumaguete City in June 1994.[151]

A Brief History and Work of the KPCT

The KPCT sent Rev. Yong-Woo Kim and family as its first missionary team to central and southern Philippines on May 21, 1989. Kim planted Shalom Presbyterian Church on March 4, 1991 and a kindergarten school at Shalom Presbyterian Church. The kindergarten school, however, closed down in April 1999, one year before Kim left for furlough in July 2000.[152]

Miss Young-Mi Kim became the second missionary of KPCT in central and southern Philippines. Young-Mi Kim arrived in Cebu City on September 26, 1990 and worked with Rev. Yong-Woo Kim in the area of children ministry. However, she started her own children ministry from January 1992 up to the present and converted it as kindergarten school in June 1992. She also planted Sae-Young Presbyterian Church and another church in Cebu City.[153]

Rev. Seong-Kook Kim joined the Visayas Presbytery of the PCP on December 8,

---

[151] Young-Ku Jee, telephone interview by the researcher, March 8, 2001.

[152] Yong-Woo Kim, telephone interview by the researcher on March 9, 2001.

[153] Young-Mi Kim, telephone interview by researcher, March 8, 2001.

1999.[154] Rev. Seong-Kook Kim was assigned in Bacolod City, Negros Occidental and planted one church in Bacolod City and its vicinity area.

A Brief History and Work of the KPCKH

KPCKH started its missionary work in central and southern Philippines in 1997. Rev. Jae-Sung Kim was the first KPCKH missionary assigned to this area and Kim and family arrived in Cebu City on March 31, 1997. Kim planted two churches, namely, the Apas Christian Church and Central Talamban Christian church, in Cebu City.[155]

An Analysis of the General Information of the Missionaries and Their Activities

In this section the researcher presents and analyzes the general information about the respondents who participated in the field survey as follows: ministerial status, age, length of work, analysis of ministry, and analysis of church growth.[156]

Table 1. Ministerial status of the missionaries

	KPCK	KPCH	KPCT	KPCKH	Total	%
Ordained pastor	6	6	1	1	14	45%
Layperson	7	7	2	1	17	55%
Total	13	13	3	2	31	
%	42%	42%	9.6%	6.4%		100%

Among the respondents, 45 % are ordained pastors and 55 % are laypersons. There are more laypersons than ordained persons because the laypersons are wives of ordained pastors plus three single laywomen missionaries. There is no single male

---

[154]Visayas Presbytery, "Souvenir Program of The 8th Stated Meeting of the Visayas Presbytery," June 6-7, 2000, Cebu Shalom Presbyterian Church, 22.

[155]Jae-Sung Kim, personal interview by researcher, January 9, 2001.

[156]The researcher constructs tables in this section based mainly on the minutes of Visayas Presbytery, directory of missionaries, personal interview, and observations.

missionary respondent in the survey.[157] The reason for this is that the Korean church does not normally ordain single men as pastors, so it is difficult for them to raise support from churches. Two single missionaries from KPCH and KPCT work with church planting and school ministry and one from KPCK works with a school ministry.

Table 2. Age range of the missionaries

Age Range	Male	Female	Total	%	Male %	Female %
31 – 40	9	10	19	61%	47%	53%
41 – 50	5	7	12	39%	42%	58%
Total	14	17	31			
%	45%	55%		100%		

The average age of missionaries is between 30 and 50, but 61% are in their 30s. The probable reasons for this age range are as follows: (1) the Korean churches' active involvement in world missions is relatively short,[158] (2) the missions history of Korean Presbyterian missions in central and southern Philippines is short compared with other area in the Philippines, and (3) Korean males must serve two to three years of military service, study in college and seminary, as well as complete a two-year internship for ordination prior to their appointment of missionary. Korean males are normally appointed later in life.

Table 3. Length of period in missions work

Period	1st term				2nd term					3rd term					4th term
Year	1	2	3	4	5	6	7	8	9	10	11	12	13	14	15
Number	2	-	2	2	2	4	1	2	3	6	2	1	2	-	2
%	19%				39%					35.5%					6.5%

---

[157]Most Korean Presbyterian churches do not allow women to be ordained, so women cannot be a senior pastor of a church. However, there are many full-time women workers in the church, called as Bible women or licensed women pastor. KPCT, however, decided to ordain women from 1995.

[158]The statistics indicate that the majority of Korean missionaries began ministry overseas in the late 1980s, just before the XXIV World Olympic Game that took place in Korea in 1988. There were only 93 missionaries in 1979, and 511 in 1986. The number increased to 3,272 in 1994. See Sang-Cheol Moon, "Current Status Quo of Korean Missionaries," *The Post Horse*, 4 (1994): 1.

Table 3 shows that 19% of the respondents are in their first term of service, 39% are in their second, 35.5% are in their third, and 6.5% are in their fourth term of service. Six point five percent have served over fifteen years. Eighty-one percent of the missionaries are in their second, third, and fourth terms, which indicate their experience and accounts for the rapid growth of church in the Philippines between 1997 and 2000.[159]

Table 4. Analysis of ministries

No	Ministries	Number of participant (Male / Female)	%
1	Church planting	26 (12 / 14)	84%
2	Theological education	14 (11 / 3)	45%
3	School ministry	7 (2 / 5)	23%
4	Student ministry	4 (3 / 1)	13%
5	Computer ministry	2 (1 / 1)	6.5%
6	Literacy ministry	2 (1 / 1)	6.5%
7	Muslim ministry	2 (1 / 1)	6.5 %
8	Medical ministry	1 (0 / 1)	3%

Table 4 shows how 84% of the missionaries concentrate on planting churches, while 45% are in theological education.[160] This may reflect the traditional understanding of the Korean church that encourages church planting and theological education in amissions setting. Sixty seven percent of single laywomen missionaries mainly engage in a church-planting ministry. As the churches grow in number, the need of national workers increase. Thus theological education is needed to train church workers. After theological educational ministry, 23 % are involved in school ministry. Missionaries start and operate a pre-school or elementary school as a means of evangelism.[161] Seventy one percent women missionaries are mainly engaged in this type of ministry. The probable reasons why women missionaries are engaged in this

---

[159]See Table 5.

[160]Tae-Yun Hwang, ed., *Directory of Korean Missions and Missionaries in the Philippines* "1999" (Manila, Philippines: The Association of Korean Missions in the Philippines, 1999), 93-376. This table was reconstructed by the researcher's manual calculation based on the directory above.

[161]The Philippine government requirements to open a school are not too strict to meet for most Korean missionaries, thus, many Korean missionaries open schools. For transportation and security reasons, most children come to the school with their mother or *Yayas* who are usually hired women for domestic works especially for taking care of children. Thus, women missionary is more accessible to children and their guardians.

ministry are (1) the easy of opening a school in a church, (2) the convenience for a missionary couple to work in the same place, and (3) the character of the work, which allows the missionary opportunity to work with children and their guardians. Thirteen percent of the missionaries work in student ministry. They evangelize in various high schools and colleges. Three out of four missionaries in this role are males. Why male missionaries prefer this ministry more than their women counterparts lies in the dynamic and active natures of the student ministry. Six and a half percent of the missionaries are engaged in computer ministry. Missionaries evangelize people by teaching computer to young people, which may not be necessarily done in a regular school environment. Six and a half percent of the missionaries are involved in literacy work.

Although many Korean missionaries show their interest in Muslim ministry, only 6.5 % of respondents are working with the Filipino Muslims in Mindanao. The possible reasons for the low percentage of workers in this area are as follows: (1) Korean missionaries have limited knowledge about the Islam religion prior to coming to the missions field, (2) Muslims have a reputation as terrorists because of the media and movies, which makes Koreans afraid of Muslims, (3) and those who want to work among Muslims also have to learn the Muslim language. Although medical ministry is well known as an effective means of evangelism, only one woman missionary nurse is participating in this area. The reason for this could be that (1) the Korean churches and missionaries prefer to focus on direct church planting rather than on indirect evangelism; (2) even the missionary nurse does not work in the medical ministry; (3) the Korean churches cannot afford to financially support the salary of medical doctors as missionaries and the facilities for such ministry; and (3) the legal constraints put on foreign medical missionary doing medical work in the Philippines.

Table 5 shows the numerical growth of the Presbyterian churches in the Visayas Presbytery from 1990 to 2000. In 1990 there were five churches, fifty baptized members, seven national workers, and six missionaries. Within ten years, the number of churches grew to sixty-four, baptized members to 1,660, national workers to forty-six, and missionaries increased to eighteen. The DGR[162] of number of church was 1,180 %, the number of baptized members was 3,220 %, the number of national workers was 500%, and the number of missionaries was 200 %. Between 1990 and 1991 the AGR[163] of the number of churches was 80 %, national worker was 43 %, and missionary was 17%. The lowest AGR of the number of church, 0 %, was between 1993 and 1994. It seems to correspond with the AGR of number of national worker and missionary in previous year, 1992-1993. The peak of AGR was between 1994 and 1995.[164]

---

[162] Decadal Growth Rate. See Table 5 and Note 29 in Chapter Two.

[163] Annual Growth Rate. See Table 5 and Note 29 in Chapter Two.

[164] The formula to calculate DGR and AGR is as follows. DGR = (the differences between 1990 and 2000) divided by the number of beginning year (1990) x 100. AGR= (the differences between the two consecutive year) divided by the number of the first year x 100. See Charles L. Chaney and Ron S. Lewis,

Table 5. Analysis of church growth (Numerical growth of Visayas Presbytery)[165]

No.	Year	Number of Church (AGR)	Number of Baptized Member (AGR)	Number of National Worker (AGR)	Number of Missionary (AGR)
0	1990	5	50	7	6
1	1991	9 (80 %)		10 (43 %)	7 (17 %)
2	1992	11 (33 %)		9 (-10 %)	11 (57 %)
3	1993	12 (8 %)	184 (268 %)	9 (0 %)	10 (-9 %)
4	1994	12 (0 %)		10 (10 %)	10 (0 %)
5	1995	23 (92 %)		21 (110 %)	13 (30 %)
6	1996	29 (26 %)		25 (16 %)	12 (-8 %)
7	1997	37 (27 %)	716 (289 %)	31 (24 %)	15 (25 %)
8	1998	39 (5 %)		28 (-10 %)	18 (20 %)
9	1999	49 (26 %)		26 (-7 %)	17 (-5 %)
10	2000	64 (31 %)	1,660 (132 %)	42 (61 %)	18 (6 %)
DGR		1,180 %	3,220 %	500 %	200%

Missions Strategies of the Korean PresbyterianMissionaries in Central and Southern Philippines

As the information section above showed, Korean Presbyterian missionaries in central and southern Philippines contributed to the growth of the church in the Philippines during the past ten years. In this section, the researcher discusses missions strategies Korean Presbyterian missionaries in central and southern Philippines employ based on their responses to the questionnaire. The researcher utilizes total weighted value, average value, and rank for analyzing the statistics.[166]

Design for Church Growth (Nashvill, TN: Broadman Press, 1977), 91-110.

[165]The researcher reconstructed this table based mainly on the journal and minutes of PCP and VP in each year. One of the most important information to measure the growth of church presents the number of baptized members. PCP and Visayas Presbytery, however, failed to collect statistical report yearly.

Strategies in Planting Church

As shown in Table 6, Korean Presbyterian missionaries in central and southern Philippines prefer the "personal evangelism" strategy (ΣWP=178 / WM=5.9 /Rank=1st), "home Bible study" (ΣWP=176 / WM=5.8 / Rank=1st), and "house worship" (ΣWP = 149/ WM=4.96/ Rank=2nd) in the early stages of church planting. Items on "contact community leaders" (ΣWP=130 / WM=4.3 / Rank=3rd) and "contact religious leaders" (ΣWP =82 / WM=3.6 / Rank=3rd) earn the third rank, which is followed by "preaching in open plaza"(ΣWP=77 / WM=2.75 / Rank=4th) and "debating with other religious scholars" (ΣWP=28 / WM=1.3 / Rank=5th).

Table. 6. Effective strategies for early stages of church planting.

What do you think are the most effective strategies for the early stages of church planting? (Please check all possible answers and rank by order of importance with 1 being the most important and 7 being the least.)

Order of importance	1	2	3	4	5	6	7				
Criteria	7	6	5	4	3	2	1	ΣF	ΣWP	WM	Rank
Personal evangelism	13	9	4	2	1	1	-	30	178	5.9	1st
Home Bible study	4	20	5	-	1	-	-	30	176	5.86	1st
House worship	5	-	15	9	1	-	-	30	149	4.96	2nd
Contact community leaders	7	1	3	7	8	4	-	30	130	4.3	3rd
Contact religious leaders	2	-	-	8	10	3	-	23	82	3.6	3rd
Preaching in open plaza	-	-	3	4	8	9	4	28	77	2.75	4th
Debating with other religion Scholars	-	-	-	-	1	4	17	22	28	1.3	5th

ΣF: Total Number of Respondent. ΣWP: Total Weighted Point. WM: Weighted Mean[167]

---

[166] The reason for utilizing "total weighted point (also called as total weighted value)", "average mean (also called as weighted value)" and "rank" for analyzing the data gathered is that it is considered the most popular, widely used, dependable, reliable measure of central tendency because all scores are counted in an adequate manner. See Leonora Loyola Oriondo and Eleanor M. Dallo-Antonio, *Evaluation Educational Outcomes (Tests, Measurement and Evaluation)* (Manila: Rex Book Store, 1984), 105. Also see Francisco A. Febre, Jr., *Introduction to Statistics* (Quezon City, Philippines: Phoenix Publishing House, 1987; reprint, 1997), 38.

[167] Hereafter, the "total number of respondents" may be referred to as ΣF, the "total weighted point,"

This outcome explains that these missionaries prefer to adopt somewhat traditional strategies in their church planting ministry. The first three strategies are commonly used methods in the Korean church, and, accordingly missionaries employ in the missions field what they have learned from their home church.

The second group of strategies, contacting community leaders and religious leaders, may reveal the Confucian background of Korean culture. It teaches that one expected to show respect to the elders of the community, and, thus obtain permission before one starts a business, a program, or other activities.

The reason why the Korean Presbyterian missionaries do not like to preach in an open plaza and debate with other religious scholars seems to come from their language problem and cultural background. Since Korean is used exclusively in Korea, Korean missionaries generally fall difficulties in learning other languages, which explains their lack of eloquence in the public area. Preaching in an open plaza does not fit the Korean Confucian cultural background. Confucianism teaches how one talk with others in a low voice. Because of the Confucian background, most Koreans are not good in reasoning with others unlike their Western counterparts who use logic and express themselves freely. Koreans generally accept the maxim, "Speech is silver; silence is golden," as one of the most valuable virtues in human relationships.

Table 7. Strategic place for church planting

What area do you think is the most strategic place for planting a church? (Please check all possible answers and rank by order of importance with 1 being the most important and 5 being the least.)

Order of importance	1	2	3	4	5				
Criteria	5	4	3	2	1	ΣF	ΣWP	WM	Rank
City (urban Area)	26	3	1	-	-	30	145	4.8	1st
Municipal town (semi-urban area)	3	21	6	-	-	30	117	3.9	2nd
Other religion dominant area	1	2	2	-	2	7	21	3.0	3rd
Rural area-barrio	-	3	15	10	-	28	77	2.7	3rd
Tribal people area	1	2	8	16	2	29	71	2.4	4th

Table 7 shows that the Korean Presbyterian missionaries in central and southern

---

as ΣWP, and "weighted mean," as "WM."

Philippines plant churches mainly in highly urbanized areas (ΣWP=145 / WM=4.8 / Rank=1st) as the most strategic place, which is followed by semi-urbanized areas (ΣWP=117 / WM=3.9 / Rank=2nd). The next items, which earned the third rank are "rural area-barrio" (ΣWP =77 / WM=2.7 / Rank=3rd) and "other religion dominant area" (ΣWP=21 / WM=3.0 / Rank= 3rd). The item on "tribal people area" received the last rank (ΣWP =71 / WM=2.4 / Rank=4th).

These missionaries have the same tendency to focus their ministry on urban areas with other Korean evangelical missionaries in other regions of the Philippines.[168] The researcher assumes some of the following reasons why Korean missionaries prefer to concentrate their ministry on urban areas: (1) the language used by most Korean missionaries in their ministry is English in that they may choose an area where English is used more widely; (2) the urban area provides more suitable education for their children; (3) the urban area has more modern technologies like telephone, computer, electricity; hospital, and others; (4) communication and information like newspapers, books, cable TV, and internet are more accessible; and (5) the biblical concept of Ishmael's offspring.

Table 8. Target group of people

What group of people is your target? (Please check all possible answers and rank by order of importance with 1 being the most important and 7 being the least.)

Order of importance	1	2	3	4	5	6	7			
Criteria	7	6	5	4	3	2	1	ΣF	ΣWP	WM	Rank
Lower class (in financial income)	9	6	4	3	2	-	-	24	137	5.7	2nd
Career group (e.g. factory workers)	7	7	7	4	2	-	-	27	148	5.5	2nd
Any people	8	-	4	1	-	-	2	15	82	5.5	2nd
Professionals	6	5	5	3	2	-	2	23	117	5	3rd
Farmers/Fishermen	1	5	6	5	-	6	-	21	99	4.7	3rd
Upper class (in financial income)	-	3	5	3	6	2	1	21	78	3.7	4th
Others											

Table 8 presents that Korean Presbyterian missionaries in central and southern Philippines do not seem to target the upper class (ΣWP=78 / WM=3.7 / Rank=4th),

---

[168]See Byung-Yoon Kim, "An Analysis of the Church Planting Methods of Korean Evangelical Missionaries in the Philippines" (Th.D. diss., Asia Baptist Graduate Theological Seminary, 1998), 109.

while the lower class is the first group targeted (ΣWP=137 / WM=5.7 / Rank=2nd). Career group (ΣWP=148 / WM=5.5 / Rank=2nd), professionals (ΣWP=117 / WM=5 / Rank=3rd), and farmers/fishermen (ΣWP=99 / WM=4.7 / Rank=3rd) are also considered target people groups. The item on "any people" (ΣWP=82 / WM=5.5 / Rank=2nd) shows the same level of interest.

Since most Korean missionaries, especially most Presbyterian missionaries hold master's degree, it seem that they prefer to work among upper class people. The survey, however, presents the opposite. They prefer to share the gospel with the lower class people more. The reasons why the missionaries choose the upper class people as their last target group may be as follows: (1) financial inferiority due to a lower living allowance, (2) lack of a good command in English and local language, (3) presumption of low receptivity of the gospel, (4) inexperience in the upper society in their home country, (5) feeling of non-homogeneity, (6) biblical concept that the rich have difficulty believing the gospel, (7) the biblical missions concept of incarnation and (8) difficulty to contact or approach. In this sense, American missionaries are successful among upper class due to their higher financial status and fluency in the English language.

Another reason could be the criticism of supporting churches. The general portrait that average Korean Christians have of missionaries is that they are skinny, hungry, ragged, endure hardships, oppressed, endure injustice, and persecuted. Even though missionaries are seen as having a difficult life they often have air conditioners, a foreign made car, a cable TV, Inter-net connection, a gas range, a cellular phone, washing machine, sofa set, and other household items. Korean missionaries are afraid of criticism from their supporting church when they come to visit the missionary. Thus, Korean missionaries prefer to work among the lower society to prove to others they are identifying with the lower class and they are practicing an incarnation life.

If these missionaries prefer to work among the economically marginal class. they may receive criticism that their ministries are simply mercy ministries, producing, the so called "rice Christians only."[169] One optimistic indication seen is that the items on "professionals," and "career group," garnered the second and third rank. Churches among these groups may have the potential to grow quickly as self-supported church.

Table 9 shows conditions Korean Presbyterian missionaries in central and southern Philippines consider in choosing an area for church planting. The following were the findings: "good receptivity of the people" (ΣWP=43 / WM=2.7 / Rank=2nd), "strategic location" (ΣWP =79 / WM=2.6 / Rank=2nd); "where the Holy Spirit guides" (ΣWP =79 / WM=3.1 / Rank=2nd); and "where no evangelical church is found" (ΣWP =77 / WM=2.6 /Rank=2nd).

---

[169]"Rice Christian" refers to believers whose faith depends on the material aids from missionaries. See Jun, *Missiology,* 242-45.

Table 9. Primary concern in choosing area for church planting

What primary concern do you think a missionary should consider in choosing an area for church planting? (Please check all possible answers and rank by order of importance with 1 being the most important and 4 being the least.)

Order of importance Criteria	1 4	2 3	3 2	4 1	ΣF	ΣWP	WM	Rank
Where the Holy Spirit guides	15	3	3	4	25	79	3.1	2nd
Good receptivity of the people	3	6	6	1	16	43	2.7	2nd
Strategic location	6	10	11	3	30	79	2.6	2nd
Where no evangelical church is found	6	11	8	4	29	77	2.6	2nd

The above survey reveals that Korean Presbyterian missionaries in central and southern Philippines do not consider any special area as the most preferable place for church planting. In general, missionaries choose a variety of places for church planting. However, the highest weighted mean (WM=3.1) lies in the item of "where the Holy Spirit guides" (ΣWP=79). It seems these missionaries are sensitive to the guidance of the Holy Spirit, yet, this is debatable because it is difficult to distinguish if the place where a missionary plants a church is exactly where the Holy Spirit guides. According to the researcher's experiences and observations, Korean missionaries mostly accept the circumstantial environment as the guidance of the Holy Spirit. For example, the local co-worker's recommendation used to be regarded as the Holy Spirit's guidance. The highest weighted mean on the item of "where the Holy Spirit guides" may represent the missionaries' attitude toward their missionary work. It may be the expression of their basic stance to obey the Holy Spirit as they carry out their tasks. Spiritual sensitivity is a strong factor in helping Korean Presbyterian missionaries choose a location for a church.

The missionaries highly value "good receptivity of the people" and "strategic location." Both items were ranked 2nd. This may indicate that these missionaries received a good orientation prior to being a church planter for the person has to analyze and identify the receptivity of the target community through a preliminary survey and to determine whether the area is accessible and has great potential.[170]

The item on "where no evangelical church is found" earns 2nd in rank. This may

---

[170] Daid J. Hesselgrave, *Planting Churches Cross-Culturally: A Guide for Home and Foreign Missions* (Grand Rapids, MI: Baker Book House, 1980), 100-106.

be because the missionaries are zealous to preach the gospel to the people. This zeal for planting a true church may have contributed to the rapid growth of the Presbyterian Church in central and southern Philippines.[171] It may also explain the Conservative background of these missionaries. It indicates that they do not acknowledge any non-evangelical group as a true church and they do not compromise with those of other heretical beliefs. It also shows that they employ an aggressive strategy in choosing a place for planting churches. It may also point out to the broad-mindedness of Korean missionaries. Their basic attitude of church planting is the same as Paul's, "I would not be building on someone else's foundation."[172]

Strategies in Preaching the Gospel

The survey in Table 10 shows the type of messages of the Korean Presbyterian missionaries in central and southern Philippines. The majority uses the item "Christ-centered message" ($\Sigma WP=145$ / WM/4.6 / Rank=1st) in their ministry. Forty-eight percent of the missionaries choose "Bible story" as one of their favorite types of messages ($\Sigma WP=57$ / WM=3.8 / Rank=2nd). The "need-focused message" ($\Sigma WP=88$ / WM=3 / Rank=3rd) and Presbyterian doctrines and beliefs" ($\Sigma WP=69$ / WM=2.7 / Rank=3rd) were chosen. "Christian ethics" ($\Sigma WP=72$ / WM=2.4 / Rank=4th) was last.

Table 10. Type of message

What type of message do you use most often? (Please check all possible answers and rank by order of importance with 1 being the most important and 5 being the least.)

Order of importance Criteria	1 5	2 4	3 3	4 2	5 1	ΣF	ΣWP	WM	Rank
Christ-centered message (e.g., cross, resurrection, redemption, etc.)	25	2	4	-	-	31	145	4.6	1st
Bible story	3	8	2	2	-	15	57	3.8	2nd
A need-focused message (e.g., healing, blessing, problem solving, etc.)	-	13	7	6	3	29	88	3	3rd
Presbyterian doctrines and beliefs	2	6	4	9	5	26	69	2.7	3rd
Christian ethics	1	2	13	8	4	30	72	2.4	4th

The fact that missionaries emphasized the "Christ-centered message (e.g.,

---

[171] See Table 5 in this Chapter.

[172] Rom 15:20.

cross, resurrection, redemption, etc.)" is relevant and appropriate because it is the essence of the gospel, especially in a Roman Catholic dominated society where the gospel seems distorted. The quality of the message determines the quality of the church especially in the pioneering stage of a church. The "Christ-centered message" may be important in building strong biblical and evangelical churches.[173]

Telling a "Bible story" is one of the well-known strategies especially among children and low-educated people. Since most Korean missionaries work among low class of people, the story-telling strategy appears effective in sharing the gospel.

More missionaries use the "need-focused message" (e.g., healing, blessing, problem solving, etc.) (WM=3) rather than the message of "Presbyterian doctrines and beliefs" (WM=2.7). Because the majority of these missionaries are from a strong Calvinistic conservative denomination, they appear to emphasize Presbyterian doctrines more than the "need-focused message" which is generally understood as non-Calvinistic. Regardless of how Korean Presbyterian Churches tolerate it, the proliferation of "need-focused message" is a growing phenomenon in the world especially in the Philippines. This universal tendency may influence the missionaries and their activities.[174]

The fact that Christian ethics is preached to a lesser extent than other types of messages does not mean it is less important. This finding may show that people pay more attention to the very essentials of the gospel. A Christ-centered message, is often preached in the pioneering stage of church work.

Table 11. Attitude toward other religion

What is your attitude toward other religions like Roman Catholic and Islam in your preaching? (Please check one only)

---

[173] M. L. Hoeges, *A Guide to Church Planting* (Chicago: Moody Press, 1973), 19.

[174] John F. MacArthur, Jr. writes "There is a discernible trend in contemporary evangelicalism away from biblical preaching and a drift toward an experience-centered, pragmatic, topical approach in the pulpit" ("The Mandate of Biblical Inerrancy: Expository Preaching," *The Master's Seminary Journal* 1, [Spring 1990]: 4). Richard L. Mayhue criticizes the modern trend of preaching as follows: "The implied conclusion is that pastors must preach what people want to hear rather than what God wants proclaimed. Such counsel sounds the alarm of 2 Tim 4:3, which warns: 'For the time will come when they will not endure sound doctrine; but wanting to have their ears tickled, they will accumulate for themselves teachers in accordance to their own desires.'" ("Rediscovering Expository Preaching" in *Rediscovering Expository Preaching: Balancing the Science and Art of Biblical Exposition*, ed. Richard L. Mayhue [Dallas, TX: Word Publishing, 1992], 6).

Attitude	Strongly hostile	Mildly hostile	Neutral	Mildly tolerant	Strongly tolerant				
Criteria	5	4	3	2	1	ΣF	ΣWP	WM	Rank
F	13	13	4	1	-	31	131	4.2	Mildly hostile
%	42%	42%	13%	3%	-				

The survey above shows the attitudes of the Korean Presbyterian missionaries towards other religions in their preaching. Forty-two percent of the respondents claimed that they were strongly hostile in their preaching and 42 % said mildly hostile. Thirteen percent of the respondents disclosed that they were neutral and only 3% were mildly tolerant.

Table11 reveals that the missionaries seem not to acknowledge religious pluralism. They may not dialogue with different religions. The fact that only 3 % of them are mildly tolerant, and no respondent is strongly tolerant of other religions, may explain why Korean Presbyterian churches send missionaries to the Philippines. Korean Presbyterian churches do not accept the biblical genuineness of the Roman Catholic Church nor do they accept the teachings of Islam and other religions.[175] Their hostility toward other religions emphasizes their theological disagreement with other religions.

Table 12 below shows the mode of how the missionaries conclude their preaching or teaching. Twenty-six percent of the respondents strongly demanded a decision from their audiences while the majority, 48 %, mildly demand a response. Another 26 % just invite the audiences to make a decision. As a whole, their mode of concluding preaching or teaching falls on the item, "mildly demand" ($\Sigma WP=93$ / WM=3.0 / Rank=2nd, mildly demand).

Table 12. Mode of conclusion of preaching

How do you conclude your preaching or teaching? (e.g., In accepting Jesus Christ as personal savior, receiving baptism, etc. Please check one only)

Attitude	Strongly demand	Mildly demand	Just invite	No mention				
Criteria	4	3	2	1	ΣF	ΣWP	WM	Rank
F	8	15	8	-	31	93	3.0	Mildly demand
%	26%	48%	26%	-				

---

[175] The theme of "The Third Kosin World Missions Conference" which took place in Kyung-Ju City, Korea on Aug. 27-30, 2000 was "The Hope of New Millennium-Jesus Christ." The conference emphasizes that there is nothing to substitute for Jesus Christ in this religious pluralism-prevailing world.

In this survey, 74 % of respondents claimed that they are demanding the audiences to make a decision at the conclusion of their preaching or teaching. This indicates that the missionaries are employing a somewhat aggressive strategy. This demanding mode may come from their modern culture.[176] This aggressive strategy does not seem to fit with the Filipino culture, namely *hiya*. Generally, when a Filipino cannot keep his or her promise, or when a sin or crime is uncovered, he or she feels a sense of shame or embarrassment-*hiya*.[177] When one feels *hiya*, he or she naturally avoids others. In this culture, when a preacher demands, strongly or mildly, that the audience make a decision, people may feel pressured to give a positive answer. It may, thus, cause them to feel *hiya* because most Filipinos have a hard time expressing a negative reaction in front of a person; yet they know they cannot keep their positive promise, which is reluctantly given because the speaker demanded it.[178] Once a missionary causes a sense of *hiya* in a group it could hinder the progress of the gospel.

Strategies in Equipping Leaders

Table 13 discloses the types of leadership training programs the Korean Presbyterian missionaries in central and southern Philippines prefer. Their first choice is "Bible school or seminary" (ΣWP=183 / WM=6.3 / Rank=1st). The next type of training they prefer is "theological education by extension" (ΣWP=165 / WM=5.5 / Rank=2nd) and "apprenticeship by missionary" (ΣWP=134 / WM=4.8 / Rank=2nd). The third types of training they prefer are "short-term training or seminars" (ΣWP=108 / WM=4.1 / Rank=3rd) and "apprenticeship by other persons who learned first" (ΣWP=88 / WM=3.8 / Rank=3rd). The last type is "correspondence course" (ΣWP=74 / WM=3.2 / Rank=4th).

Table 13. Appropriate leadership training program

What type of leadership training program do you think is appropriate in your context? (Please check all possible answers and rank by order of importance with 1 being the most important and 7 being the least.)

---

[176] Unlike ancient Koreans, modern Koreans act very impatiently in every way. "Patience and Perseverance" were the two typical words, which described the character of old Koreans. However, the progress of modern technology has changed the life style of modern Koreans. See Donald MacIntyre, "Wired for Life," *Time*, 11 December 2000, 18-23.

[177] The English term for *hiya* is embarrassment, timidity, modesty, or shyness (Evelyn Miranda-Feliciano, *Filipino Values and Our Christian Faith* [Manila: OMF Literature Inc., 1990], 40).

[178] Ibid., 39-41.

Order of importance Criteria	1 7	2 6	3 5	4 4	5 3	6 2	7 1	ΣF	ΣWP	WM	Rank
Bible school, seminary	16	9	2	1	1	-	-	29	183	6.3	1st
Theological education by extension	5	14	6	2	2	1	-	30	165	5.5	2nd
Apprenticeship by missionary	6	4	6	5	4	3	-	28	134	4.8	2nd
Short-term training or seminars	1	1	10	6	5	3	-	26	108	4.1	3rd
Apprenticeship by other persons who learned first	2	1	2	9	4	5	-	23	88	3.8	3rd
Correspondence course	-	1	4	3	6	9	-	23	74	3.2	4th

The survey shows that the missionaries chose Bible school or seminary more than other type of training programs to equip the national leadership in the church. The researcher assumes that it reflects their own experiences in Korea. Because most of these missionaries have received their theological training in a well-organized institutions, theological college or theological seminary in Korea, they may not be familiar with other types of training methods. This explains why they have one traditional type of theological institution in each of the four major missions stations in central and southern Philippines respectively. The second largest number of the missionaries are involved in this traditional approach to educating pastors in ministry.[179]

These missionaries chose the items on "theological education by extension" and "apprenticeship by missionary" as their second choice for training local leaders in the church. No missionary, however, currently employ this method for equipping people. The reasons why none of them is successful may be as follows: (1) they were not trained in this method, (2) they do not receive appropriate orientation in how to use this method before they are dispatched, (3) they lack the ability to speak English or the local language, and (4) when they attempt to use this method, they use Korean methods which cause conflict in the ministry setting.[180] Even though none of them are successful in this method as mentioned above, the fact that these two items had a higher rank (Rank=2nd) reveals a preference for this method. The high cost of theological education in a regular institution, the difficulties of inter-islands communication and transportation caused by geographical distances, and the difficulty of finding teachers may cause missionaries to consider seriously "theological education by extension" or "apprenticeship by missionary" as an alternative way of training

---

[179]The locations of the four institutions are Cebu Bible College in Mandaue City, Cebu; Dumaguete Bible College in Dumaguete City, Negros Oriental; Hosanna Bible School in Iloilo City, Iloilo; and Presbyterian Bible College in Davao City.

[180]See the "Introductory" section of page 7.

leaders.

The reason for not considering the item, "correspondence course," is uncertain. If geographical distances make it difficult for students to commute between church and school, the correspondence course may be a good substitute.[181] The most probable reason for this seems that missionaries and national workers do not have much information about this program. Another possible reason why missionaries do not prefer this method lie in a bad impression of correspondence studies in Korea.[182]

Table 14. The period of held leadership

How long do you think a missionary should hold the leadership of the church? (Please check one only)

Period	Until the church elects one elder	Until the church can support itself	Until a Filipino pastor can lead	Until the missionary leaves				
Criteria	4	3	2	1	ΣF	ΣWP	WM	Rank
F	1	8	22	-	31	72	2.3	Until a Filipino pastor can lead
%	3%	26%	71%	-				

The table above shows the appropriate period of leadership a missionary expects to hold leadership in a local church. Three percent of respondent chose the item "until the church elects one elder" and 26% prefer "until the church can support itself." The biggest percentage of the respondent chose "until a Filipino pastor can lead" and no one selected the item, "until the missionary leaves." As a whole, the Korean Presbyterian missionaries prefer the response "until a Filipino pastor can lead" (ΣWP=72/WM=2.3 / Rank=3rd, until a Filipino pastor can lead).

In this table, the survey revealed that most missionaries plan to relinquish their

---

[181] Most Korean Presbyterian missionaries in central and southern Philippines want their co-workers who are studying in theological seminary or other institution to come back to church every weekend for Sunday ministry. But the inter-island transportation is its biggest hindrance.

[182] Theological correspondence courses in Korea are generally known as anomalous because their academic standard is considered low, the study period is too short, and the ordination is too rapid. Thus, most churches do not acknowledge the credibility of those institutions and people who completed such courses and are ordained by the same institutions.

leadership to a national leader. It may also indicate how missionaries wait cautiously for a proper time to transfer leadership. The researcher assumes that these missionaries do not consider the election of a church elder as the proper time to transfer leadership. This seems reasonable because an elder is still a layperson according to the Presbyterian Church government, and is thus, deemed immature to serve as a spiritual leader of a congregation.[183]

Even when a church can support itself financially, there is some question as to whether this is a good time to turn the church over to a national leader. Apparently, it seems more desirable for a local church to have their own national leadership for the congregation than to depend on the leadership of a foreign missionary. There is no reason for a local church to postpone inviting a mature leader, if the local church has adequate means of support. The fact that no respondent chose the item, "until the missionary leaves" indicates the healthy attitude of the missionaries not to dominate the church in their missions field.

Table 15. Qualification of being a pastor

What qualification do you consider when you choose a pastoral leader or a co-worker? (Please check all possible answers and rank by order of importance with 1 being the most important and 7 being the least.)

Order of importance	1	2	3	4	5	6	7				
Criteria	7	6	5	4	3	2	1	ΣF	ΣWP	WM	Rank
Calling from God	23	5	1	-	1	-	-	30	199	6.6	1st
Faithfulness	4	3	4	3	1	3	1	19	88	4.6	3rd
Strong spirituality	2	5	10	2	3	3	1	26	118	4.5	3rd
Gifted and trained for leadership	2	6	3	5	2	5	1	24	102	4.2	3rd
Theological Background	-	2	8	7	4	2	1	24	97	4	4th
Teachableness	-	3	2	4	7	3	6	25	77	3	4th
Team spirit	-	5	-	3	5	3	7	23	70	3	4th

---

[183]In general, Presbyterian government divides two types of elder. The first is the teaching and ruling elder, pastor, and the second is the ruling elder, commonly called, "elder." The tasks of the teaching elder, pastor, are preaching, teaching, ruling, and all others in the church, while the ruling elders are not expected to preach and teach. (Gerardo H. Kim, ed., *Presbyterian Government* [Quezon City, Philippines: Presbyterian Church of the Philippines, 1995], 5-8).

Table 15 explains what qualifications the Korean Presbyterian missionaries consider important when they choose a national co-worker. The highest ranked qualification they choose was "calling from God" (ΣWP=199 / WM=6.6 / Rank=1st). The next highest ranked qualifications are as follows: "strong spirituality" (ΣWP =118 / WM=4.5 / Rank=3rd), "gifted and trained for leadership" (ΣWP=102 / WM= 4.2 / Rank=3rd), "theological background" (ΣWP=97 / WM=4 / Rank=3rd), and "faithfulness" (ΣWP=88 / WM=4.6 / Rank=3rd). The lowest ranked choices are: "teachableness" (ΣWP=77 / WM=3 / Rank=4th) and "team spirit" (ΣWP=88 / WM=3/Rank=4th).

The Korean Presbyterian missionaries in central and southern Philippines consider "calling from God" as the most important element in being a leader of a church. This may reflect the importance of a "calling from God" in their own lives in Korea. This calling from God may have been made clear through their five to nine years of theological training in the seminary and practical ministry training under supervision of senior ministers. Their ministries in central and southern Philippines are additional evidence of their "calling from God."[184] The researcher, thus, assumes that these missionaries' emphasis on a "calling from God" is critical to the strategy of missionary work and in choosing leadership in the local church.

The items, "teachableness " and "team spirit" were considered important as a qualification of a leader. According to the researcher's observation and experiences, almost all Korean missionaries have very strong personalities. They hardly accept advice from a senior even if the later hold substantial ministry experiences. Most Korean missionaries have a tendency to learn from their own experiences, not from others even though they know it is the best way to save time and resources. Therefore, "team spirit" is not a major concern when they choose their co-worker.[185]

Table 16 reveals the degrees of how the Korean Presbyterian missionaries in central and southern Philippines utilize women leadership in their ministries. Eighty-four percent of these missionaries appear to be positive in mobilizing women leadership in the church. Forty-five percent put limit on ordination and serving as a senior pastor in a local church, while 39 % agree to allow women's ordination and pastoring in a senior capacity. Sixteen percent reply that women leadership must never be practiced in the church. As a whole, these missionaries in central and southern Philippines prefer to utilize women leadership in the church, except ordination and the senior leadership (ΣWP=100 / WM=3.2 / Rank=excluding ordination and senior pastorate).

---

[184]See C. A. Clark, *The Work of the Pastor* (Seoul: Korea Christian Publishing, 1981), 23-28.

[185]This idea may be traced to the influence from old Confucianism. The Confucian philosophy sees the hierarchy structure as important so it is automatically assumed that a senior or the one in position teaches the others. The young generation point, thus, may oppose the seniors because of the lack of mutual sharing of leadership, which the Filipino culture accepts.

Table 16. Women leadership

How much do you think the women-leadership should be practiced in the Philippine church setting? (Please check one only)

Women leadership	Including ordination and senior pastorate	Excluding ordination and senior pastorate	Never	Not Sure				
Criteria	4	3	2	1	Σ	ΣWP	WM	Rank
F	12	14	5	-	31	100	3.2	Excluding ordination and senior pastorate
%	39%	45%	16%	-				

Thirty-nine percent preferred the item on "including ordination and senior pastorate." This seemed revolutionary to the researcher. The reasons for this openness may be in the following: (1) The influence of the Filipino culture that the leadership of women in the home and community is highly esteemed and practiced;[186] (2) In every aspect of human life in the modern world, women participate actively; (3) It is a rebellious spirit of the young generation against the old fossilized generation; (4) The influence of feminism; (5) The influence of some denominations that allow women ordination and senior pastorate; (6) Churches see how God uses women in leadership in the Scriptures; and (7) The lack of qualified male leadership in some local churches in the Philippines. The policy of the PCP, however, does not allow women ordination.

The survey in Table 16 may reflect the traditional character of Korean Presbyterian churches. Among the four groups of the Korean Presbyterian Church that sent missionaries to the Philippines, only one group (KPCT) has ordained a woman pastor recently and the other three groups refused to do so. Sixteen percent of respondents chose "never," which proves the conservative stance of the Korean Presbyterian Church. Beside the biblical foundation, one reason for the extreme

---

[186]There are three theories about women leadership in a Filipino home. The first is that the mother or wife may share in the exercise of authority and decision-making, but the man of the house almost always has the final say. The second is that Filipino society is basically matriarchal; the husband is merely a nominal position. He is allowed to be the figurehead, but actually it is the wife, the woman who is dominant. The third is more of a shared reciprocal venture rather than either solely male or female-dominated. This leadership pattern has its roots in the past, as equality of men and women is an ancient Malay tradition that has withstood Muslim influences in Indonesia and Spanish Catholic traditions in the Philippines (Evelyn Miranda-Feliciano, 52-53).

conservative stance of Korean Presbyterian Church could be the strong Confucianism dominant culture in Korea. Women are seen not as valued as men and are considered inferior.

Table 17. Ideal length of missionary service

How long do you think is the ideal period for a missionary to serve in the missions field? (Please check one only)

Length of service	Life-time	Above 20 years	15-20 years	10-15 years	5–10 years	1-5 years	ΣF	ΣWP	WM	Rank
Criteria	6	5	4	3	2	1				
F	7	7	12	4	1	-	31	139	4.4	Above 20 years
%	22%	22%	39%	13%	3%	-				

Table 17 shows what the Korean Presbyterian missionaries in central and southern Philippines consider the ideal length of missionary service in the missions field. Thirty-nine percent reply "15-20 years" as the ideal length. Twenty-two percent respectively chose the items on "life time" and "above 20 years." Thirteen percent of the respondents answered "10-15 years," and 3 %, "5-10 years." As a whole these missionaries deem "above 20 years" ($\Sigma WP=139$ / WM=4.4 / Rank=above 20 years) as the ideal length of missionary service in the missions field.

The survey in Table 17 may reflect the commitment of these missionaries to their work, alongside the Korean churches' expectation of their workers. Despite the Western trend of missionary commitment of getting shorter, the survey shows how respondents prefer long-term service, which is the traditional view of their Korean-based church.[187] The two items on "life time" and "above 20 years" are about the same idea. If one male missionary comes to the missions field when he is thirty years old and serve more than twenty years, he is to be almost sixty years old. This is not a good age to begin a new work in his home country.[188] In addition to the above fact, the item "15-20 years" is also near to life time service. Consequently, the three items are almost

---

[187]Leslie Pelt, "What's Behind the Wave of Short-termers?" *Evangelical Missions Quarterly* 28 (October, 1992): 385.

[188]A Korean male ordained missionary could hardly go to the missions field before the age of thirty. The required minimal education for regular study takes twenty one years: elementary six years, middle school three years, high school three years, college four years. Seminary takes three years and internship for ordination two years. Additional is the three-year military service. Therefore, if a boy starts elementary school when he is six years old, he can be ordained when he reaches thirty.

the same so, 83 % prefer the "life time" service on the missions field.

On the contrary, Scott Bessenecker suggests that short-term missions like what Paul did in Acts is possible today.[189] Bessenecker presents the following five reasons why short-term ministries are possible: (1) English is the most widely spoken language in the world today as Greek was in the first century; (2) Travel along the Roman roads enabled Paul to reach vast areas. Likewise, travel today is fast, cheap, far-reaching, and widely available; (3) In Paul's days, Hellenistic culture predominates the world. Today, Westernization of the world helps begin dialogue; (4) Mystery religions which indicate inward spiritual hunger as in Paul's days, is also seen in the New Age movement today; and (5) Paul visited Synagogue as a starting point. Likewise, the university campuses often the open door to a hostile environment today. The researcher anticipates that the Western trend of short-term missions may become popular in Korea sooner or later.[190]

Table 18. Principles for a new missionary to follow

What principles should a new missionary need to follow? (Please check all possible answers and rank by order of importance with 1 being the most important and 5 being the least)

Order of importance	1	2	3	4	5				
Criteria	5	4	3	2	1	ΣF	ΣWP	WM	Rank
Following the guidance of the Holy Spirit through the church	11	15	3	2	-	31	128	4.12	2nd
Waiting until the time when the direct guidance of the Holy Spirit comes	17	2	2	4	4	29	111	3.82	2nd
Following the guidance of senior missionaries	-	9	8	7	4	28	78	2.78	3rd
Following the guidance of the leaders of the church or missions agency	1	4	12	8	5	30	78	2.6	4th
Following own decision after long consideration	2	1	6	5	12	26	54	2	4th

---

[189]Scott Bessenecker, "Paul's Short-term Church Planting: Can It Happen Again?" *Evangelical Missions Quarterly* 33 (October 1997), 330-31. See also Lud Golz, "If Paul Got Organized to Reach His Objectives, So Can You," *Evangelical Missions Quarterly* 27 (July 1991): 268-72.

[190]Many prominent missions leaders in Korean church have traditional concept of missionary, lifetime service. They used to criticize short-term missions such as O.M. International. One of the reasons was that Western missions agencies recruited Korean young short-term missionaries and used them for auxiliary work only.

Table 18 shows what guidance new Korean Presbyterian missionaries in central and southern Philippines take in their early stages of missionary work. The item on "following the guidance of the Holy Spirit through the church" ranked the first place (ΣWP=128 / WM=4.12 / Rank=2nd). The next "waiting until the time when the direct guidance of the Holy Spirit comes" (ΣWP=111 / WM=3.82 / Rank=2nd) was second. The item on "following the guidance of senior missionaries" came in third place (ΣWP=78 / WM=2.78 / Rank=3rd). The fourth place were two items on "following the guidance of the leaders of the church or missions agency" (ΣWP=78 / WM=2.6 / Rank=4th) and "following own decision" (ΣWP=54 / WM=2 / Rank=4th).

The survey on Table 18 reveals that these missionaries prefer the guidance of the Holy Spirit rather than the guidance of leaders. These missionaries, however, chose "the guidance of the Holy Spirit through the church" more than "the direct guidance of the Holy Spirit." The fact that "waiting until the time when direct guidance of the Holy Spirit comes" took second place in rank is unpredictable in the Presbyterian Church and may indicate that these missionaries could be influenced by Pentecostalism both in Korea and in the Philippines.

Table 19. Gifts for missionaries

What gifts do you think are important for missionaries? (Please check all possible answers and rank by order of importance with 1 being the most important and 8 being the least)

Order of importance Criteria	1 8	2 7	3 6	4 5	5 4	6 3	7 2	8 1	ΣF	ΣWP	WM	Rank
Faith	17	6	4	1	1	1	-	-	30	214	7.13	1st
Ministry (serving people)	4	9	9	4	3	-	-	-	29	181	6.24	2nd
Discerning of spirit	5	7	7	4	1	2	1	-	27	163	6.03	2nd
Prophecy (preaching or teaching the Bible)	8	4	6	4	3	-	1	2	28	164	5.85	2nd
Exhortation	1	1	2	6	8	4	4	2	28	111	3.96	3rd
Giving (mercy)	1	-	1	6	4	4	4	4	24	84	3.5	4th
Healing power	1	1	1	-	4	9	9	-	25	82	3.28	4th
Speaking in tongue	1	2	-	1	1	2	3	14	24	57	2.37	5th

Table 19 shows gifts that these missionaries consider important for missionaries. These missionaries chose the item on "faith" as the most important (ΣWP=214 / WM=7.13 / Rank=1st). The second items were "ministry (serving people)" (ΣWP=181 / WM=6.24 / Rank=2nd), "discerning of spirit" (ΣWP=163 / WM=6.03 / Rank=2nd), and "prophecy (preaching or teaching the Bible)" (ΣWP=164 / WM=5.85 / Rank=2nd). The third was "exhortation" (ΣWP=111 / WM=3.96 / Rank=3rd). The fourth was "giving (mercy)" (ΣWP=84 / WM=3.5 / Rank=4th) and "healing power" (ΣWP=82 / WM=3.28 / Rank=4th). The fifth was "speaking in tongue" (ΣWP=57 / WM=2.37 / Rank=5th).

The survey in Table 19 reveals that these missionaries reflect the traditional character of the Presbyterianism as shown by the high ranking of the items on "faith," "ministry (serving people)," "discerning of spirit," and "prophecy (preaching or teaching the Bible)." When compared with the survey in Table 18 the item on, "direct guidance of the Holy Spirit" which ranks second, the items on "healing power" and "speaking in tongue" with low in ranking are unexpected to the researcher. Evidently, respondents seem to attempt holding on to their Presbyterian identity, and yet, trying to be open to learn about the charismatic movement at the same time.

Strategies in Financing the Ministry

Table 20. Effectiveness of direct financial support

What do you think of a national church leader supported by Korean church directly? (Please check one only)

Effectiveness Criteria	Effective 3	Not sure 2	Ineffective 1	ΣF	ΣWP	WM	Rank
F	10	1	20	31	52	1.67	Ineffective
%	32%	3%	65%				

Table 20 shows the effectiveness of direct financial support to the national leaders from the missionary sending church in Korea. Thirty-two percent of respondents claim it as "effective," while 65 % note its ineffectiveness. Three percent are not sure. As a whole, the Korean missionaries in central and southern Philippines consider the direct support to the national leaders of the church from the missionary sending church in Korea as "ineffective" (ΣWP=52 / WM= 1.67 / Rank=ineffective).

The researcher agrees with the result of the survey, the direct support to the national church reader from abroad is ineffective. The biggest problem the researcher observes is the envy of other national church leaders who do not have direct financial support from abroad. This jealousy hinders good relationships among national church leaders and drives them to find the same financial privileges. Wayne Allen presents some of the following negative points when national church leaders receive subsidies from abroad. He presents: (1) The initiation of subsidy signals a move away from reliance on lay leadership to reliance on a professional clergy; (2) The paid workers focus more on pleasing the paying agency than on meeting the needs of the churches; (3) When the local church realize their pastor receives foreign subsidy, they lose their sense of ownership of the pastor.[191] Interestingly, the survey concludes that it is the direct support from abroad for national leader that is ineffective, not the support itself from abroad.

Table 21. The effectiveness of "self-support" principle

How effective do you think is the "self-support" principle in Philippine setting from the beginning of the church? (Please check one only)

Effectiveness Criteria	Effective 3	Not sure 2	Ineffective 1	ΣF	ΣWP	WM	Rank
F	20	3	8	31	74	2.38	Effective
%	64%	10%	26%				

The above survey reveals how the Korean Presbyterian missionaries in central and southern Philippines consider the effectiveness of the "self-support" principle in their present working setting. Sixty-four percent of respondents consider it "effective" while 26 % note it "ineffective". Ten percent of them claim it as unclear. On the average, these missionaries regard the "self-support" principle as "effective" (ΣWP=74 / WM=2.38 / Rank=effective).

The "three self formula," i.e., self-support, self-govern, and self-propagation, is deemed to be the most probable direct cause of rapid and healthy growth of the church among Korean church leaders and Korean missionaries. Most Korean Presbyterian missionaries are psychologically and physically expected to apply this principle in their ministries. Likewise, the Korean churches supporting Filipino churches expect the latter to become self-supporting.

The researcher, however, assumes that the "self-support" principle is ideal, but not

---

[191] Wayne Allen, "When the Mission Pays the Pastor," *Evangelical Missions Quarterly* 34: 2 (April 1998): 176-81.

practical in Philippine setting. Table 22 shows how missionaries want to be fully supported by their sending church, not by self-supporting or tent making. Table 23 reveals how missionaries spend most of their missions funds for the salary of their coworkers, operating institutions, and constructing building. In the Visays Presbytery, for instance, lesser than 20 % of churches are self-supporting. Thirty-six percent of respondents chose "not sure" or "ineffective," which shows the dilemma the missionary respondents are facing.

Table 22. Types of missionary in financial support

Regarding financial support, what type of missionary do you think is effective in your setting? (Please check all possible answers and rank by order of importance with 1 being the most important and 7 being the least.)

Order of importance	1	2	3	4	5	6	7				
Criteria	7	6	5	4	3	2	1	ΣF	ΣWP	WM	Rank
Fully supported by sending church	21	4	1	2	-	-	-	28	184	6.5	1st
Partially supported; living by sending church, project by hosting church	5	11	4	3	-	-	-	23	133	5.7	2nd
Partially supported; living by tent-making, project by sending church	2	3	14	2	-	-	-	21	110	5.2	2nd
Self-supporting or tent-making	2	5	2	11	-	-	-	20	98	4.9	2nd
Fully supported by host church	-	-	-	1	-	-	-	1	4	4	3rd
Partially supported; living by host church, project by sending church	-	-	-	-	1	-	-	1	3	3	4th
Others	-	-	-	-	-	-	-				-

Table 22 presents the most effective type of missionary in regards to financial support. The Korean Presbyterian missionaries in central and southern Philippines rank "fully supported by sending church" ($\Sigma WP=184$ / WM=6.5 / Rank=1st) as the most effective type of missions support. Ranked second include the items, "partially supported; living by sending church, project by hosting church" ($\Sigma WP=133$ / WM=5.7

/ Rank=2nd), "partially supported; living by tent-making, project by sending church" (ΣWP=110 / WM=5.2 / ank=2nd), and "self-supporting or tent-making" (ΣWP=98 / WM=4.9 / Rank=2nd). Two items "Fully supported by host church " and "Partially supported; living by host church, project by sending church," seem out of discussion.

Survey indicates that respondents prefer to be supported by their home church in Korea, including their living allowance and project funds. Only one respondent chose the item on "fully supported by the host church" as the 4th ranked option. This may reveal that none of these missionaries could not depend on local funds for adequate support. Only one respondent selected "partially supported; living by host church, project by sending church" as his/her fifth rank in the order of importance. These two cases prove the insufficiency of funds in the local church to support a missionary. It may explain why missionaries expect their living allowance to come, at least in part, from the sending church or even by tent-making, instead of simply depending on the host church.

The item on "partially supported; living by sending church, project by hosting church" appears to be what the Korean church consider desirable according to the "three self formula." What is unclear, however, is the reason behind ranking it second by respondents as missionaries know that local churches cannot afford yet the funds for a project, like constructing the church building.

In brief, the missionaries discern that the local churches have difficulty in supporting the missionary's living allowance or supporting any project. Facing reality in the missions field, the sending churches or agencies in Korea could be requested to reconsider the "three self formula," since it may take time to apply it in the early stages of the work.

Table 23 reveals how the Korean Presbyterian missionaries in central and southern Philippines allocate missions funds. Missions funds are primarily allocated for "co-worker's salary" (ΣWP=199 / WM=6.86 / Rank =1st). The item on "operating institutions" (ΣWP=132 / WM=5.73 / Rank=2nd) ranks second. Next in the missionary investment include "building construction" (ΣWP=129 / WM=5.16 / Rank=3rd), "rental" for residential house or worship place (ΣWP =113 / WM=4.91 / Rank=3rd), "evangelism" (ΣWP =100 / WM=4.54/Rank=3rd), "equipping ministry" (ΣWP =100 / WM=4.54 / Rank=3rd), and "scholarship for youth" (ΣWP =87 / WM=5.11 / Rank=3rd). The fourth area where funds are used is "compassionate ministry" (ΣWP =71 / WM=3.55 / Rank=4th).

Table 23. Use of missions funds

Regarding missions funds, where do you use them mainly? (Please check all possible answers and rank by order of importance with 1 being the most important and 8 being the least.)

Order of importance Criteria	1 8	2 7	3 6	4 5	5 4	6 3	7 2	8 1	ΣF	ΣWP	WM	Rank
Co-worker's salary	12	9	2	5	-	1	-	-	29	199	6.86	1st
Operating institutions	3	8	5	3	-	1	1	2	23	132	5.73	2nd
Building construction	10	1	1	2	4	1	1	5	25	129	5.16	3rd
Scholarship for youth	1	4	2	4	3	1	2	-	17	87	5.11	3rd
Rental	1	4	10	-	1	2	2	3	23	113	4.91	3rd
Equipping ministry	1	3	3	4	5	2	3	1	22	100	4.54	3rd
Evangelism	3	-	6	2	2	6	1	2	22	100	4.54	3rd
Compassionate ministry	-	1	-	5	6	-	7	1	20	71	3.55	4th

The fact that most missionaries (ΣWP =29) subsidize "co-worker's salary" indicates that most local churches are not yet self-supporting. Although establishing a self-supporting church is considered as one of the primary goals of church planters, the Korean Presbyterian missionaries in central and southern Philippines cannot neglect the co-worker's salary at the early stage of church planting. The researcher agrees with the idea of two missiologists, William J. Kornfield, who points out that financial paternalism need to be avoided, and Harvie M. Conn, who criticizes, from a biblical perspective, the "self-support myth" as it robs the missionary sending churches and host churches of the joy of mutual giving.[192]

Missionary respondents appear to stress the use of indirect evangelism because "operating institutions" receives second ranking. The items that ranked third are "rental," "scholarship for youth," "building construction," and "equipping ministry." These are all indirect evangelism. Why "evangelism" is ranked lower is unclear. The researcher assumes it is because of the missionaries' difficulty in English and other local languages.

The fact that "compassionate ministry" has the lowest rank does not indicate that missionaries are "stingy" as many of them prefer to work among the lower class.[193] It may reveal that the missions funds for these missionaries are too limited to extend their ministry to this area because the other needs like salary for the co-workers, could be more urgent.

Table 24 explains the appropriate period to support a newly planted church financially. In this survey, no item is ranked prominent. Twenty-seven percent of the respondents prefer the item "until it can fully support itself." Twenty-four percent

---

[192] See Footnote 76 in Chapter One.

[193] See Table 8 in Chapter Two.

choose the item "until it has 50-70 baptized members." Twenty percent claim "maximum first 5 years" are enough. Thirteen percent thought the church needs outside aid "until it has its own church building and parsonage." Three respondents favor support for a "maximum first 7 years." As a whole, the Korean missionaries in central and southern Philippines prefer to support a newly planted church "until the church can support itself (ΣWP=149/WM=4.9/Rank=until it can fully support itself).

Table 24. The appropriate length of financial support

How long do you think is it appropriate to support a church financially? (Please check one only)

	F	%	Criteria	ΣF	ΣWP	WM	Rank
Until it has 50-70 baptized members	7	24%	7				
Until it has its own church building and parsonage	4	13%	6				Until it can fully support itself
Until it can fully support itself	8	27%	5	30	149	4.96	
Maximum first 5 years	6	20%	4				
Maximum first 7 years	3	10%	3				
Maximum first 10 years	1	3%	2				
Others	1	3%	1				

a. According to the achievement degree of the master plan for being self-supporting

The survey shows the Korean Presbyterian missionaries in central and southern Philippines are paternal in supporting churches. Each missionary wants to take care of the church until it becomes financially able. Each respondent chooses different items respectively, so which reflects the idea of preferring full self-support. Those respondents, for example, who choose the item "until it has 50-70 baptized members" may assume that if a church has 50 to 70 baptized members, it could support itself. Respondents who choose "maximum 5 years" may share in the same assumption. All other respondents, therefore, seem to have the same assumption that the periods they choose are appropriate for self-support.

Strategies in Team Ministry

Table 25 reveals how effective these missionaries work together on the missions field. Sixty-one point three percent of respondents answered that their work together was "effective," while 29 % claim that their work together is "very effective." Six point five percent judge it as "ineffective," and 3.2 % choose the item "not sure." As a whole, the Korean Presbyterian missionaries in central and southern Philippines consider their work together as effective (ΣWP=128 / WM=4.13 / Rank=effective).

Table 25. Effectiveness of cooperation

How effectively do you think missionaries work together? (Please check one only)

Criteria	F	%	ΣF	ΣWP	WM	Rank
Very effective	9	29%				
Effective	19	61.3%	30	128	4.13	Effective
Not sure	1	3.2%				
Ineffective	2	6.5%				
Very ineffective	-	-				

The above survey shows that missionaries accept the biblical model of cooperation.[194] The fact that over 90 % of them agree that their cooperation in missions work is "effective" indicates a bright future for cooperative missions work. KPCH missionaries in Davao City, apparently, seem good in cooperation with fellow missionaries in all area of their ministries currently. They choose one senior missionary as supervisor and entrust four missionaries, according to their gifts, to cover the following four departments: theological education, church planting, students and youth ministry, and administrative ministry. Each department develops both short and long-term plans for the missions which are presented at a missions meeting. The plans accepted at the meeting are carried out in cooperation with all the missionaries under the leadership of each department head with a senior supervisor.

The other missionaries in other regions of central and southern Philippines also work cooperatively, but on a more limited basis. Most of them, however, work alone in a church planting area, although they tend to cooperate in other areas like theological education, medical ministry, church administration, and student and youth ministry. The reason why 6.5 % of them answered it is "ineffective" seems to lie in their failure to map out missions goal as a team. Another reason could be traced to the missionaries' lack of experience in the field.

---

[194]Eccl 4:12 states, "Though one may be overpowered, two can defend themselves. A cord of three strands is not quickly broken" (NIV).

Table 26. Helpfulness of short-term missionary

Do you think a short-term Korean missionary (one or two year) can be helpful for your ministry? (Please check one only)

Helpfulness Criteria	Yes 3	No 2	Not sure 1	ΣF	ΣWP	WM	Rank
F	7	6	18	31	51	1.6	Not sure
%	22%	20%	58%				

The survey in Table 26 shows how the Korean missionaries consider the feasibility of the short-term missionary. Fifty-eight percent claim they are "not sure." Twenty-two percent respond with "Yes," while 20 % choose "No." Obviously, seventy-eight percent are somewhat negative (ΣWP=51 / WM=1.6 / Rank=not sure) on the matter of the helpfulness of short-term missionaries in their ministries.

The fact that most of these missionaries are negative about the helpfulness of a short-term missionary, may reflect the basic understanding of their home churches concerning a short-term missionary. Generally, candidates for short-term missionaries are young people, and they are hardly accepted as missionaries in most Korean Presbyterian churches. Two probable reasons could be noted thus: (1) the downward trend of national economic status from 1997 to 2000 in Korea, and (2) the influence of Confucian philosophy that gives lesser value to the youth.[195]

Short-term volunteer, however, is a worldwide trend.[196] Therefore, Korean church and missionaries may need to listen to some Western missiologist like Michael Pocock's ideas about how to reap long-term rewards from short-term investments. These are as follows: (1) promoting identification with the missions, (2) pre-selection factors promote career involvement, (3) significant ministry, (4) competent field

---

[195] One example is the M/V Doulos of Operation Mobilization. Missionaries on the M/V Doulos are basically short-term workers. When the boat visited Cebu City, Philippines in 1993, there were more than 30 young Korean short-term missionaries. This number was the biggest number from one nation on the boat. However, there were only eight Korean short-term missionaries, including one Korean-American from the States, when the same boat visited in Cebu on April, 2001. This decrease in number seems temporary. When the Korean economic status recovers, the number may increase soon.

[196] The worldwide tendency of missions, Leslie Pelt diagnosed in 1992, is that the number of full-time missionaries has decreased and the number of short-time missionaries increased from 1980s. He predicted that sixty-six percent of all missionaries in the world would be short-term missionaries by the year 2000, if the increasing rate of short-term missionary between 1985 and 1988 continues (384).

coordinators, (5) post-field debriefings, and (6) the alumni association.[197]

Table 27. Level of cooperation

How much do you work together with other missionaries? (Please check one only)

Criteria	F	%	ΣF	ΣWP	WM	Rank
Cooperation in all ministries	8	26.7%				
Mostly in cooperation (above 70%)	6	20%	30	98	3.27	Half and half
Half cooperation, half individual	5	16.6%				
Mostly individual (above 70%)	8	26.7%				
No cooperation	3	10%				

Table 27 reveals the degree of cooperation that missionaries have with others. Twenty-six point seven percent claim they work cooperatively in all ministries, and 20 % note that they cooperate with others (above 70% of their ministries). Sixteen point six percent choose the item "half cooperation, half individual." Another 26.7 % claim they work individually in most of their ministries (above 70% of their ministries) and 10 % say they only work individually. Evidently, the missionary respondents operate within a work "half in cooperation and half individually" policy (ΣWP=128 / WM=3.27 / Rank=half cooperation and half individual).

The survey in Table 27 shows that 90 % of the Korean Presbyterian missionaries in central and southern Philippines work with other missionaries in their ministries. Some cooperate minimally in their ministries. Only 10 % do not cooperate with other missionaries. From their experiences of cooperation, they evaluate their cooperation as effective in Table 25. Although 90 % see their cooperation as effective in Table 25, 46.7 % of them claim to have worked cooperatively with other missionaries in most of their ministries (above 70%) in table 27. The researcher assumes the reasons why only minorities of them work together as follow: The transportation and communication problems, which are caused by the geographical distances in central and southern Philippines, and the unclear missions goal as a team.

Of the 10 % who choose the item, "no cooperation" in Table 27 corresponds with the number of those who choose the two items "not sure" (3.2 %) and "ineffective" (6.5 %) in Table 25. The reasons for working individually could be stated

---

[197]Michael Pocock, "Gaining Long-term Mileage from Short-term Programs," *Evangelical Missions Quarterly* 23 (April 1987): 154-60.

thus: (1) they may be new missionaries with little ministries, (2) they are missionaries who are alone on one island or in a remote place, (3) the character of their ministries may be professional or no other person has interest in it, and (4) other reasons such as personal character.

Table 28. Authority to make decision

In making decision, who holds the authority between you and your national co-worker(s)? (Please check one only)

Criteria	F	%	ΣF	ΣWP	WM	Rank
Flexible according to the situation and cases	18	58.1%	31	84	2.7	Half and Half Excluding financials
Half and half including financials	7	22.5%				
Half and Half excluding financial	3	9.67%				
National co-worker alone including Financials	2	6.45%				
Missionary alone	1	3.2%				

Table 28 shows how authority much the Korean Presbyterian missionaries in central and southern Philippines share with their national co-workers with regard to decision making. Fifty-eight point one percent claim that they are "flexible according to the situation and cases." Twenty-two point five percent register on item, "half and half including financials," while 9.6 % chose "half and half excluding financials." Six point four percent answer that they gave full authority to their "national co-worker including financials." Only 3.2 % reply that the missionary alone holds full authority. As a whole, these missionaries share the authority to make decision "half and half excluding financials" (ΣWP=110 / WM=3.54 / Rank= half and half excluding financials) with their national co-workers.

According to the survey on Table 28, the majority of the missionaries (58.1%) seem flexible in the matter of sharing authority on decision-making with their national co-workers, although this area seems ambiguous. It may mean that the national co-workers are dependent on the decision of missionaries. It is not far from the item that "missionary alone" (3.2%) holds the authority to make decisions. Nine point six percent missionaries prefer to give equal authority to their national co-workers, but not about financial matters.[198] In brief, the three items "half and excluding financials,"

---

[198]The researcher asserts that if a missionary holds the authority to control the finances exclusively, all

"flexible according to the situation and case," and "missionary alone" are basically the same. Thus, the majority (71%) of the Korean Presbyterian missionaries in central and southern Philippines are not willingly to share power to make decisions with their national counterparts.

The authority to control finances does not mean one holds the bank book or cash. It means that one has the authority to make the budget. Table 28 reveals that only 28.9 % missionaries who chose the items "national co-worker alone including financials" and "half and half including financials" have the desire to share the authority to make decision with their national co-workers.

Table 29. Understanding and participating of support churches

How much do you feel your supporting churches understand your ministries and participate in it? (Please check one only)

Criteria	F	%	ΣF	ΣWP	WM	Rank
Partially understand, partially participate	16	51.6%	31	110	3.54	Fully understand, partially participate
Fully understand, fully participate	8	25.8%				
Fully understand, partially participate	4	12.9%				
Not sure	3	9.68%				
Minimal understand, minimal participate	-	-				

The survey in Table 29 shows how much the supporting churches understand the ministries of these missionaries and participate in it. Fifty-one point six percent respond that supporting churches understand and participate partially. Twenty-five point eight percent note that supporting churches understand fully and participate fully. Twelve point nine percent choose the item "fully understand, partially participate." Nine point six percent say they are "not sure." As a whole, the supporting churches understand the ministries of the Korean Presbyterian missionaries in central and southern Philippines fully and participate in it partially (ΣWP =110 / WM=3.54 / Rank=fully understand, partially participate).

In missions work, understanding and getting the participation of the supporting churches are two vital factors. God is the initiator of missions and He continues it

---

other authority that the missionary gives to the national co-workers are meaningless because the one who controls the purse string may still control the rests.

through the church. Therefore, without the church's understanding and participation in missions, missions is impossible.[199] Though it is hard to identify the criterion of what it means by full or partial understanding of missions, 51.6 % of the missionary respondents feel their supporting churches understand missions partially and thus, churches participate partially. It may reflect the reality of that the Korean church faces in missions today. More Korean churches need to be encouraged to participate in missions.

In brief, this survey reveals the Korean churches' poor understanding of missions. Survey shows that 38 % claim that their supporting churches understand missions fully, and that 62 % claim that their supporting churches understand missions partially. Although Korean churches claim they are the second in the number of missionaries they send to the world, they need to improve their understanding of missions.[200]

Strategies in Contextualized Communication

Table 30. Languages employed for ministry

What language(s) do you use mainly in your ministry? (Please check all possible answers and rank by order of importance with 1 being the most important and 4 being the least.)

Order of importance	1	2	3	4	ΣF	ΣWP	WM	Rank
Criteria	4	3	2	1	ΣF	ΣWP	WM	Rank
English	18	12	-	-	30	108	3.6	1st
Cebuano (Visayas)	13	14	-	-	27	94	3.48	1st
Ilongo (Hiligaynon)	-	3	-	-	3	9	3	2nd
Tagalog	-	-	1	-	1	2	2	3rd

Table 30 shows what language the Korean Presbyterian missionaries in central and southern Philippines employ mainly in their ministry. English (ΣWP =108 / WM= 3.6 / Rank=1st) is the first choice. Cebuano comes next (ΣWP =94 / WM=3.48 / Rank-1st), the dominant language in central and southern Philippines. The third is Ilongo (Hiligaynon) (ΣWP =9 / WM=3 / Rank=2nd) and Tagalog (ΣWP =2 / WM=2 /

---

[199] Tai-Woong Lee, *The Theory and Practice of Korean Missions* (Seoul: GMF Press, 1994), 223.

[200] Steve S. C. Moon, "The Acts of Koreans: A Research Report on Korean Missionary Movement," available from http://www.krim.org.files/ The_Acts_of_Koreans.doc: Internet; accessed 3 December 2001.

Rank=3rd), the national language, is the least chosen language.

The largest number of the Korean Presbyterian missionaries in central and southern Philippines employ English as their first medium of language in their ministries. Since Korea is a mono-language country; most Koreans have no chance to attain proficiency in English. Therefore, it is not surprising that English is the first barrier to overcome for most Korean missionaries when they learn a specific local language in mission field. The second reason why these missionaries adopt English as their main medium to communicate with people is that the period of learning English takes too long and it is difficult to begin another language. The third reason is that English is the official language, and its use is widely accepted among all people groups in the Philippines. The researcher, therefore assumes that if English is the medium only to learn the specific local language, all these missionaries have to learn an appropriate local language by which they could communicate with the local people.

Although English is the main medium of communication with people, many of these missionaries extend their time to master a specific local language, e.g., Cebuano or Ilongo. The researcher assumes that most missionaries learn the language of the specific area in which they minister. Most missionaries used Cebuano, 9.6 % use Ilongo as second medium, and 3 % learn Tagalog. This should correspond with the missionaries in respective language area.

Most of the Korean Presbyterian missionaries in central and southern Philippines employ English and at least one local language together to communicate with the people. This is an effective strategy. If the national language (Tagalog) is used in places where a minority language is best understood by the people, a segment of people within the Christian church might be linguistically neglected. Though the government encourages people to adopt the national language, using the local language in sharing the gospel is critical to understand better national concerns.[201]

Table 31. Degree of emphasizing "Korean style"

How much do you think a missionary can emphasize "Korean style" in his or her ministry? (Please check one only)

Degree of emphasis	Always	Often	Seldom	Never				
Criteria	4	3	2	1	ΣF	ΣWP	WM	Rank
F	-	8	20	3	31	67	2.16	Seldom
%	-	26%	64%	10%				

---

[201] Carol V. McKinney, "Which Language: Trade or Minority?" *Missiology* 18 (July 1990): 289.

The survey in Table 31 shows how much these missionaries employ the practices of their home church, Korean style, in their ministries. Sixty-four percent of them emphasize "seldom," 26 % do it often, and 10 % never emphasize it. On the average, missionaries "seldom" practice Korean style (ΣWP=67 / WM=2.16 / Rank=seldom) in their ministries.

Some of the Korean Presbyterian missionaries in central and southern Philippines emphasize "Korean styles" in worship, Bible study, church administration, communion, prayer, ceremonies, constructing church building, among others. The reason for this lies in financial paternalism, or the ethno centric attitude that the "Korean style is better."[202] The researcher assumes that there is a connection between Korean missionaries' financial paternalism and the emphasis of "Korean style." The greater the funding from Korean church, the higher the danger of spreading a Koreanized gospel and activities in the church. Many local congregations and church leaders grumble about the missionaries' emphasis on "Korean style" murmuring, "We are not Koreans." The fact that 26 % stress "Korean style often" and 64 % emphasize it "seldom," indicates that the Korean Presbyterian missionaries in central and southern Philippines are somewhat ethnocentric.

Table 32. Frequency to observe "Thanksgiving Sunday"

How often do you observe "Thanksgiving Sunday" in a year? (Please check one only)

Frequency of observing Thanksgiving	Once a year in November	Twice a year in June & Nov.	Three times a year	Never				
Criteria	4	3	2	1	Σ	ΣWP	WM	Rank
F	27	2	-	2	31	116	3.74	Once a year in Nov.
%	88%	6%	-	6%				

Table 32 shows how often the missionary respondents in central and southern Philippines observe "Thanksgiving Sunday" in a year. Eighty-eight percent observed it once a year in November. Six percent chose the item "twice a year in June and November." Another six percent answered they never observe "Thanksgiving Sunday."

---

[202]William J. Konfield, "What Hath Our Western Money and Our Western Gospel Wrought?" *Evangelical Missions Quarterly* 27 (July 1991): 233. In this article, Konfield, as a Western missionary, warns the Westernization of the gospel with a strong voice.

The fact that nearly all missionaries, 94 %, observe "Thanksgiving Sunday" in November, and 6 % observe it one more time in June, reveals that these missionaries observe exactly the same practice back Korea.[203] The researcher sees it as an improper practice because the months of June and November belong to the planting season rather than the harvest seasons in central and southern Philippines. Furthermore, barley and wheat are not cultivated in tropical zone like the Philippines. Comparing Table 31 and 32, 90% of the Korean Presbyterian missionaries in central and southern Philippines who emphasize "Korean style" often or seldom appear to be part of the 94% of the missionaries who observe "Thanksgiving Sunday" in November and June. The researcher understands the reason why most of these missionaries, 94 %, observe it in November as this month eliminates the agricultural elements and stresses the gifts and presents one receives from God during the year.[204] Since most Presbyterian churches in central and southern Philippines are located in urban or semi-urban area, and people residing in urban or industrialized area are not familiar with agriculture, these missionaries seem to apply the modern concept of "Thanksgiving Sunday" in their church.

One thing that is not clear to the researcher is that there are no missionaries who observe "Thanksgiving Sunday" three times a year, and 6 % never observe it. Since farmers in central and southern Philippines harvest rice three times a year, it would not be strange to have three "Thanksgiving Sundays" in a year. The researcher assumes that if Presbyterian churches which are located in agricultural areas observe "Thanksgiving Sunday" three times a year following the agricultural calendar in the Philippines, this practice may enhance the faith of the congregation greatly.

Table 33 shows the special occasions these missionaries observe in their church. The most observed special occasion is "Thanksgiving service" (94%). The second Group, comprising between 70 % and 90 %, registers "church anniversary" (87 %), "Christmas day service" (77 %), "New Year worship" (77 %), and "Easter dawn union worship with other churches as a special place" (74 %). The third group, between 50% and 70% takes "Good Friday noon service" (68 %) and "Last night of the year service" (52 %). The fourth group (50%) points to "Christmas Eve service" (45 %), "Parent's Sunday service in May" (42 %), and "Children's Sunday service in May" (32 %). The least is "Barley and wheat harvest Thanksgiving service" (6 %).

---

[203] Traditionally, Korean churches observe two "Thanksgiving Sunday" in a year. The first is in June, after the harvest of barley and wheat, and the second is in November for harvesting rice, fruits, and all other crops.

[204] Joo-Chae Jung, "Life of Thanksgiving" (sermon preached at the Jamsil Central Church in Seoul on 21 November 1999), Cebu Bible College Library, Mandaue City, Philippines. Although most urban Christians are not connected with agriculture directly, Thanksgiving in November is agreeable with the agricultural calendar. Thus, The Korean church's Thanksgiving in November may still be valid within the context.

Table 33. Special occasions observed

What special occasions do you observe in your church? (Please check all that you observe in your church in the Philippines)

Criteria	F	ΣF	%
Thanksgiving service	29		94%
Church anniversary service	27		87%
New Year worship Service (even it is not on Sunday)	24		77%
Christmas-day service	24		77%
Easter dawn union worship with other churches at a special place	23		74%
Good Friday noon service	21	31	68%
Last night of the year service	16		52%
Christmas Eve service	14		45%
Parent's Sunday service in May	13		42%
Children's Sunday service in May	10		32%
Barley (Wheat) harvest thanksgiving service	2		6%

The survey explains how the Korean Presbyterian missionaries in central and southern Philippines unconsciously import "Korean style," which was mentioned in Table 31. Among the second group items that post a percentage between 70 % and 90 %, there are two out of four items that are somewhat foreign in the Filipino churches. These are "New Year worship service even it is not on Sunday," and "Christmasday service."[205] Though "Mother's day" is observed in the church, children's Sunday in May" is not observed in the Philippines. The researcher may assert that there are some special occasions that the missionaries practice in their church which do not originally belong to the Filipino church.[206]

---

[205]Because of fire cracking the previous midnight, Christmas morning and New Year day morning, Filipinos are used to waking up late, and do not have any special activities the next morning. "Christmas Eve service" and "last night of the year service" are not practiced as church activities, but communities are involved in fire cracking. Churches have Christmas parties several days earlier than Christmas

[206]Missionaries may need to adopt some missiological principles regarding contextualization in their ministries such as what David Racey presents. He suggests the following five principles regarding contextualization: "(1) If your conscious does not bother you practice it, then it must be legitimate; (2) If your approach to contextualization goes against the views of other missionaries, it must be illegitimate; (3) Your approach to contextualization must be accepted by the local standard; (4) Your approach to contextualization must not contradict with the essential truths of the Bible; (5) Contextualization is just a

Table 34 shows the activities the Korean Presbyterian missionaries in central and southern Philippines implement in their ministries. The most practiced items of activities that received over 70 % are "tithe" (F=27 / Rate=87 %), "Wednesday evening prayer meeting" (F=26 / Rate=84 %), and "simultaneous prayer in loud voice" (F=23 / Rate=74 %). The second group of items that were ranked between 50 % and 70 % were "Sunday evening service" (F=21 / Rate=68 %), "regular visitation of member's house" (F=20 / Rate=65 %), "whole congregation retreat" (F=19 / Rate=61 %), "occasional thanksgiving offering" (F=18 / Rate=58 %), and "cell group prayer meeting" (F=16 / Rate=52 %). The third group of items that were ranked below 50 % was "dawn prayer meeting" (F=14 / Rate=45 %), "Friday vigil prayer meeting" (F=13 / Rate=42 %), "Revival meeting" (F=10 / Rate=32 %), "whole member attending Sunday" (F=10 / Rate=32 %), "Sunday evening commitment service" (F=7 / Rate=23 %), and "fasting prayer meeting" (F=6 / Rate=19 %).

Table 34. Activities implemented in the church

What activities do you implement in your ministries?
(Please check all that you practice in your church)

Criteria	F	ΣF	%
Tithe	27		87%
Wednesday evening prayer meeting	26		84%
Simultaneous prayer in loud voice	23		74%
Sunday evening service	21		68%
Regular visitation of member's house	20		65%
The whole congregation retreat	19		61%
Occasional thanksgiving offering	18		58%
Cell group prayer meeting	16	31	52%
Dawn prayer meeting	14		45%
Friday vigil prayer meeting	13		42%
Revival meeting	10		32%
The whole member attending Sunday	10		32%
Sunday evening commitment service	7		23%
Fasting prayer meeting	6		19%

means to an end" ("Contextualization: How Far is Too Far?" *Evangelical Missions Quarterly* 32, [July 1996], 306-9).

All items on Table 34 are traditionally well known, and are widely practiced activities for the growth of a church in Korean context.[207] Some of them like "dawn prayer meeting" and "revival meeting" are well known strategic activities in Korean church. Other items contributed also greatly to Korean church growth, which encourage the missionaries to practice them in their ministries. The item that received the highest percentage (87 %) is the tithe. If missionaries utilize the concept of "Utang na loob" for tithe and other occasional thanksgiving offering, it could bring about a tremendous result. "Utang na loob" is an interior law which dictates the recipient of a good act or deed to behave generously towards his or her benefactor as long one lives. To a Filipino, showing a lack of due gratitude toward his or her benefactor is unacceptable. One's sense of "Utang na loob" defines his or her integrity as a person in the context of social relationship.[208]

"Simultaneous prayer in loud voice" is a current phenomenon that has spread in the Pentecostal or charismatic churches in the Philippines. Traditionally, Filipinos were peace-lovers. They used to speak in low voice and not shout.[209] Though "simultaneous prayer in loud voice" is a growing phenomenon among some Filipino churches, Korean missionaries expect not to force people to adopt it just because they are familiar with this style of prayer.

Fasting appears as one of the weakest points in the Filipino life. Generally, Filipinos like to have fellowship seating around the eating table. They usually eat five to seven times daily. In this culture, one could hardly imagine days without food even it is for certain religious purposes.[210] "Regular visitation of members' house" including

---

[207]To examine each items on Table 34, the researcher held a small council with three Cebu Bible college students and two elementary school teachers of Jewels Christian Learning Center at the dinning hall of Cebu Bible College on May 18, 2001. All the attendees were Filipinos except the researcher. In the session, everybody expressed their experiences, feelings, views, and perspectives about Filipino cultures, customs, values, traditions, and viewpoints. The researcher examined the adequateness of each item on Table 34 respectively and used the collected knowledge from the said session.

[208]Tomas Quintin D. Andress and Pilar Corazon B. Ilada-Andres, *Making Filipino Values Work for You* (Makati, Philippines: St. Paul Publications, 1986), 32-33. If Filipino Christians understand God correctly and accept Him as their best benefactor in their heart, one can expect they bring their tithes to the church and thus, churches can be self-supported soon. There is, however, a negative side to "Utang na loob." It may create a kind of dependency that is detrimental to the formation of the people. If people misunderstand the church as the representative of God on earth or constant benefactor, they would be the recipients who are endlessly soliciting helping. Missionaries, thus, may need to teach them the correct gospel first before they emphasize tithes and offerings.

[209]One Korean group of mainly pastors and their wives visited Bradford Church (UCCP), one of the oldest churches, on Jones St., Cebu City in 1990. During the prayer time, members of the Korean group prayed so loudly that all the Filipino congregations ceased their prayer, but watched Koreans with astonishing eyes. Reverend Patricio Ezra, the senior pastor of the church, shared his experience with the researcher by saying, "I could not finish even one sentence of my prayer because of their noise."

[210]Filipinos like table fellowship in general. They usually eat five to seven times daily: get a hot chocolate or other hot drink after wake up, breakfast, snack, lunch, snack, supper, and snack before going

a non-members' house, is always welcomed. The hospitality of a Filipino is celebrated in the world. Missionaries, therefore, may employ this strategy for evangelism more actively.

The "dawn prayer meeting" is another appropriate activity for Filipino congregation because Filipinos rise early. The researcher assumes that more religious people get up earlier. Devoted Roman Catholics have their own style of dawn prayer processions. Missionaries, thus, may encourage people to attend a daily dawn prayer meeting and use this strategy for developing the faith of their congregation.

Table 35 reveals how often the missionaries use Filipino poems, idioms, current issues, stories, legends, epigrams or other literary forms in their sermons or teachings. Sixty-two percent of the respondents claim that they use these literary devices seldom, 32 % claim that they used them often, and 3 % choose them "frequently." On the whole, the missionaries use them seldom. (ΣWP=72 / WM=2.4 / Rank=seldom).

Table 35. Frequency of using Filipino literary forms

How often do you use Filipino poems, idioms, issues, stories, legends, epigrams or other literary forms in your sermons or teachings? (Please check one only)

Frequency of use Criteria	Frequently 4	Often 3	Seldom 2	Never 1	Σ	ΣWP	WM	Rank
F	1	10	19	-	30	72	2.4	Seldom
%	3%	32%	62%	-				

From the above survey in Table 35, the researcher concludes that the Korean Presbyterian missionaries in central and southern Philippines need to improve in the commitment to contextualizing the message. Sixty-two percent of the respondents seldom employ these literary forms, which may indicate that their messages or teachings may not be easy to understand for a Filipino audience.[211] Missionaries need to be deeply immersed in the local cultures to understand the people more and thereby, mobilize all possible elements of the cultures for a more meaningful communication of the gospel.[212]

---

to bed.

[211]One example of this in the story of the "Peace Child" among the Sawi tribe in Irian Jaya. In this book, Don Richardson explains that God prepares already "redemptive analogies" with which people can understand the gospel more easily and correctly in every culture. Therefore, the job of missionaries is to find the hidden analogies and apply it to the biblical truth (*Peach Child*, trans. Jichan Kim [Seoul: Word of Life Press, 1987], 4).

[212]Kathleen D. Nicholls appeals for communicating the gospel through traditional poetry, music,

Summary of the Chapter

This chapter presents the survey results of missions strategies of the Korean Presbyterian missionaries in central and southern Philippines. A total of thirty-one respondents representing four missions agencies of the four Korean Presbyterian groups participated in the survey. Answers to the questionnaires were tabulated, tallied, compared, analyzed, and explained.

The first part of this chapter focused on basic information about the respondents. A brief history of the four missions agencies and statistics were researched through various original written materials, interviews, letters, and personal diaries. The information gathered through questionnaires revealed the respondents' status, ages, length of period in missions work, and analysis of ministries. The survey presented an analysis of numerical church growth in the Visayas presbytery under which the Korean Presbyterian missionaries in central and southern Philippines work together.

The second part of this chapter focused on the strategies employed by the Korean Presbyterian missionaries in central and southern Philippines in their missions work according to the following order: (1) strategies in planting church (2) strategies in preaching the gospel, (3) strategies in equipping leaders, (4) strategies in financing the ministry, (5) strategies in team ministry, and (6) strategies in contextualized communication. The survey showed the struggle of the Korean Presbyterian missionaries in central and southern Philippines in these six areas of ministries. Majority of respondents pointed to language barrier and cultural adjustments as two of the biggest problems in their ministries. The survey also revealed that many of them stay within the boundary of the conservative stance of their home church, while others tend to adopt some novel strategies in their ministries. Despite the lack of cross-cultural experiences and preparation before their arrival on the missions field, the Korean Presbyterian missionaries in central and southern Philippines managed to plant churches and baptized, new members.

---

drama, puppetry, dance, and painting. She says, "Music, drama, dance, poetry, and others are part of our lifeblood and not a cultural museum piece ("Tell the Story Powerfully in Local Cultural Forms," *Evangelical Missions Quarterly* 19 [October 1983]: 299).

Chapter Three

AN ANALYSIS OF MISSIONS STRATEGIES OF THE KOREAN PRESBYTERIAN MISSIONARIES IN CENTRAL AND SOUTHERN PHILIPPINES IN THE LIGHT OF PAUL'S MISSIONS STRATEGIES

The focus of this research has been the missions strategies that the Korean Presbyterian missionaries in central and southern Philippines employed in their ministries. Chapter One of this study investigates Paul's missions strategies which are revealed in Acts 13-28 as the foundational principles for missions strategies of all ages. In Chapter Two, the missions strategies employ by the Korean Presbyterian missionaries in central and southern Philippines are presented based upon field survey. In this chapter, the strengths and weaknesses of the missions strategies employed by Korean Presbyterian missionaries in central and southern Philippines will be identified and analyzed in the light of Paul's missions strategies.

Areas of strength and weakness were chosen on the basis of the missions strategies employed by the Korean Presbyterian missionaries in central and southern Philippines in Chapter Two. Criteria to judge the strengths and weakness were based on either correspondence with or difference from the foundational principles of Paul's missions strategies examined in Chapter One. The formula of strength is as follows:A (i.e. Paul's missions strategies) affirms B (i.e. missions strategies used by the Korean Presbyterian missionaries in central and southern Philippines) is "strength." The formula of weakness will be as follows: A (i.e. Paul's missions strategies) affirms that B (i.e. missions strategies used by the Korean Presbyterian missionaries in central and southern Philippines) is "weakness."[213]

Areas of Strength

There are seven identifiable areas of strength in missions strategies. Each of these strengths will be elaborated and analyzed.

Table 36. Strengths of missions strategies

☐	High zeal for evangelism
☐	Strong spiritual sensitivity
☐	A robust identity
☐	Persistent effort to equip national leadership
☐	Partnership responsibility for new churches
☐	Willingness to cooperate
☐	Endeavor to adopt local culture

High Zeal for Evangelism

The survey shows that the Korean Presbyterian missionaries in central and southern Philippines demonstrate a high level of evangelistic fervor. This affirms Paul's emphasis on testifying to the gospel of God's grace and fulfilling the Great Commission of the Lord.[214] In Paul's ten years ministry, he plants numerous churches in urban commercial and socio-political centers of the eastern half of the Roman Empire. It follows that urban areas have a greater concentration of people who could hear the gospel. Paul preaches only of Jesus' cross, his resurrection, repentance, and the need for salvation. He rejects truth claims of other religions and strongly opposes religious pluralism. He presents the gospel clearly and demands people to make a decision quickly for Christ. Paul does not hesitate to preach about anything that would

---

[213]Byung-Yoon Kim, "An Analysis of the Church Planting Methods of Korean Evangelical Missionaries in the Philippines" (Th.D. diss., Asia Baptist Graduate Theological Seminary, 1998). 164.

[214]When Jesus gave the Great Commission (Matt 28:18-20; Mark 16:15; Luke 24:47-48; John 20:21), Paul was not a recipient. He, however, had a strong conviction that he received the same Great Commission in Acts 20:24.

help people know more about Christ. He preaches publicly and does house to house visitation (20:20).

Chapter Two showed that respondents and their national co-workers baptized 1,660 persons and planted sixty-four churches in the past ten years.[215] This figure shows a high growth rate of the Presbyterian Church in both central and southern Philippines. The high growth rate indicates the zeal for evangelism on the part of the missionaries. The respondents' zeal for evangelism is also observed in the process of choosing a location for planting a new church.[216] They prefer urban or semi-urban areas for planting a new church. Table 10 shows these respondents claim "Christ-centered message (e.g., cross, resurrection, redemption, etc.)" as their preferred type of message, thereby affirming their strong evangelistic-orientation in church planting strategies. Their attitude toward other religions of these respondents is also evangelistic. Eighty-four percent of the respondents claimed that they reject the truth-claims of other religions. However, 13 % claim that they are neutral, with 3 % saying they are mildly tolerant.[217] This shows how missionaries reject religious pluralism, which teaches that non-Christian religions are alternative ways to salvation.[218] These missionaries, thus, include all people of other religions as their prospective people for evangelism. The missionaries' high zeal for evangelism appears in their preaching and teaching. At the conclusion of the preaching, 74% of the respondents would make an appeal to the audience to make a decision to accept Jesus as personal Savior, or to receive baptism; 26% would invite people to make a decision.[219] This high percentage of encouraging people to make decision shows a strong evangelistic orientation of the Korean Presbyterian missionaries in central and southern Philippines. Evidently the high zeal for evangelism contributes to the rapid growth of the church in areas where missionaries work.

Strong Spiritual Sensitivity

Another perceived area of strength in missions strategies that the Korean Presbyterian missionaries in central and southern Philippines employed is spiritual sensitivity. Maintaining spiritual sensitivity in the missions field is one of the most difficult things for missionaries because of satanic attack, depression from language learning, differences in weather and culture, food problems, endemic diseases, and

---

[215]See Table 5 in Chapter Two.

[216]See Table 7 in Chapter Two.

[217]See Table 11 in Chapter Two.

[218]Ho-Jin Jun, *Religious Pluralism and Mission Strategy for Other Religions* (Seoul: The Korea Society of Reformed Faith and Conduct, 1992), 46.

[219]See Table 12 in Chapter Two.

other factors.

In Paul's missions strategies, sensitivity to the guidance of the Holy Spirit is crucial. When he moves to Macedonia, Paul and his team think it is the Holy Spirit who leads them to that area (16:10). In addition to the direct guidance of the Holy Spirit, Paul accepts the decision of the church leaders as something that echoes the guidance of the Holy Spirit.[220] Paul has a strong conviction that it is God's calling that leads him to preach the gospel to the Gentiles.[221]

In the same vein, almost 50% of the respondents choose the item, "where the Holy Spirit guides," as a primary concern in choosing an area for church planting[222] The area of church planting is chosen on the basis of a perceived guidance of the Holy Spirit, over against the "good receptivity of the people," "strategic location," and "where no evangelical church is found." The respondents consider "calling from God" as the most important qualification, with "strong spirituality."[223] These missionaries prefer the guidance of the Holy Spirit rather than the guidance of human leaders of the church. There is, however, the tend to choose "the guidance of the Holy Spirit through the church" more than "the direct guidance of the Holy Spirit."[224] When they consider the necessary gifts of the Holy Spirit for missionary work, they choose "discerning of spirit" as one of the top four gifts.[225]

According to Table 30, 77% of the respondents observe "New Year worship Service (even if it is not on Sunday)," 32% observe, "children's Sunday service in May," 6% observe "barley (wheat) harvest thanksgiving service," 77% observe "Christmas-day service," and 52% observe "last night of the year service." These occasions are not generally observed in Filipino churches. Forty-five percent of the respondents practice "dawn prayer meeting," 19% "fasting prayer meeting," 23% "Sunday evening commitment service," 32% "the whole member attending Sunday," 58% "occasional thanksgiving offering," and 74% "simultaneous prayer in loud voice."[226] The Korean missionaries in central and southern Philippines seem to practice these activities in their planted churches with the thought of improving

---

[220] Paul follows the decision of the leaders of Antioch church (Acts 13:1-3) and the decision of the elders of Jerusalem church, and considering them as equal guidance from the Holy Spirit (Acts 15:28-31). Beside Paul, his missions team members also accept the "vision of a man of Macedonia" which Paul alone saw in the night as the guidance of the Holy Sprit (Acts 16:9-10).

[221] Acts 20:24; 22:15, 21.

[222] See Table 9 in Chapter Two.

[223] See Table 15 in Chapter Two.

[224] See Table 18 in Chapter Two.

[225] See Table 19 in Chapter Two.

[226] This style of prayer was uncommon in traditional Korean Presbyterian churches before the Pentecostalism was introduced.

spiritual sensitivity among church members, as Korean churches normally do.

The survey, therefore, shows the Korean Presbyterian missionaries in central and southern Philippines are sensitive to the spiritual aspect of their ministries. Even though they acknowledge some activities are foreign for the Filipino congregations, they implement those activities because they expect that the activities may help the national congregations be sensitive to the Holy Spirit and the growth of churches.

Holding Robust Identity

The emphasis on strong "identity" in the missions field is one perceived strength in the missions strategies of the Korean Presbyterian missionaries in central and southern Philippines. Respondents claim to have a strong identity as missionaries.

Similarly Paul's conviction about his identity as called by God is evident in his speeches to the priest of Zeus and the people in Lystra (14:15), to the philosophers at Areopagus (17:16-31), and to the king, Agrippa and governor Festus (26:29). Before Agrippa and Festus, he boldly declares, "All who are listening to me today may become what I am, except for these chain" (26:29). Paul rejects religious pluralism, but strongly hold the position that Jesus is the only solution and he is His messenger. He has the ability to discern which ministry is genuine and which is not. Paul denies the false teachers from Judea and accuses them in front of the elders in Jerusalem (15:1-2). He, however, accepts other churches and people even though he never meet them before (28:14, 15).[227]

Traditionally Korean Presbyterian churches have not accepted the biblical genuineness of the Roman Catholic Church as well as Islam and all other religions.[228] The Korean Presbyterian missionaries in Central and southern Philippines follow this theological position in their dealing with adherents of other religious traditions. If they accept religious pluralism, they would lose their foundation for missions. Missionary respondents seem to discern whether or not these churches adhere to sound biblical teachings.[229] The Korean Presbyterian missionaries in central and southern Philippines

---

[227]In his epistle to the church in Rome prior to his visit, Paul asks for financial support for his travel to Spain (Rom 15:24).

[228]Eu-Pyo Hong, *Present-Day Churchly Trends* (Daegu, Korea: Bo Mun Publishing Co., 1979), 143-47. Hong classifies Roman Catholic Church as one of heretics. See also these missionaries' hostile attitude towards other religions in their preaching and teaching on Table 11 in Chapter Two.

[229]In general, the basic tenets of the evangelicals are as follows: (1) belief in the full authority of Scripture (its inerrancy), (2) the necessity of personal faith, (3) the individual's conversion, and (4) the strong commitments to the importance of evangelism (Mark Ellingsen, *The Evangelical Movement* [Minneapolis, MN: Augsburg Publishing House, 1988], 46). The definition of evangelicalism, however, is

normally plant new churches where no evangelical church is found.[230]

The outcome of discussing important gifts or talents for missionary work confirmed the missionaries' strong Presbyterian identity.[231] This is evident as the items on "faith," "ministry (serving people)," "discerning of spirit," and "prophecy (preaching or teaching the Bible)" were ranked high, while the items on "healing power" and "speaking in tongue," were marked low. Field survey seems to indicates that strong conviction regarding Presbyterianism is one factor that enhances missionary to achieve church growth in central and southern Philippines.

Persistent Effort of Equipping National Leadership

One of the most important responsibilities of a missionary, especially if the missionary is a foreigner, is transferring leadership of the churches to local leaders. In an attempt to plant an indigenous local church, the Korean Presbyterian missionaries in central and southern Philippines make every effort to transfer the leadership of the church to local leaders. Prior to the transferring of leadership, leaders are nurtured and equipped. This, of cause, has a basis in Paul's ministry.

In Miletus, Paul strives to preach the gospel and to teach and equip the believers to be matured (20:20). He also establishes a Bible institute and teaches people for three years. He teaches people by making himself a model in how to serve the Lord. Paul also equips women to serve as ministry leaders, and letting them disciple others (18:20). In his desire to produce local leaders, Paul hands over ministries to local leaders within a given period of time.

Likewise persistent efforts on the part of Korean missionaries to transfer leadership to the local leaders are noted in field survey results. In fact, the missionaries establish four theological institutions in each of their major missions stations for equipping local leaders.[232] This number of institutions is the biggest among the four Presbyteries of the General Assembly of the Presbyterian Church of the Philippines.

Normally the Korean missionaries desire to hold the leadership of the church until they leave it for other ministries. Though they do not consult with each other about the

---

unclear in Korean church yet. It is understood sometimes as a synonym for Reformed faith or conservatism (Hyung-Ki Lee, "Historical Origin of Evangelical Theology and Evangelical Reformed Theology in Korea, " in *Bible and Theology vol. 1,* ed. Korean Evangelical Theological Society [Seoul: Jung Eum Publishing Co., 1983], 183-98). See also Hong 42-7.

[230]See Table 9 in Chapter Two.

[231]See Table 19 in Chapter Two.

[232]See Table 13 and Footnote 41 in Chapter Two.

proper time to transfer leadership, they do concur that the leadership of the church needs to be handed over to local leaders.[233] Thus, only 3.2% of the respondents claim to hold the authority in the church to make decisions. In this case, the researcher assumes that the missionary may be new and has no national co-worker yet. On the contrary, 6.4% of the respondents claim that they would transfer all the authority to make decisions, including financial matters, to the local leaders.[234] The rest are in the process of entrusting the authority to make decisions to their local counterparts.

Partnership Responsibility for New Churches

God does not only want all people to be saved, but also to become responsible members of the church. The new converts need to grow until they become mature. So, a missionary expects to evangelize people and nurtures them.

Paul spends time and energy caring for new converts. He revisits churches, plants, comforts, and encourages new believers. He writes letters to communicate to new believers, and give instructions to messengers to bring back news from the churches. Paul's commitment to maintain responsibility over new believers is far excellence.

The Korean Presbyterian missionaries in central and southern Philippines share with Paul in terms of caring for their converts. The respondents claim that they would support the newly planted church until it becomes a self-supporting body.[235] Although there are pros and cons for financial support and its methods, the missionaries' partnering attitude to take care of the newly planted church is noticeable. Missionary respondents want to hold on the leadership of the church "until a national pastoral leadership can lead the church fully." In this partnering responsibility model, missionaries cling on to their authority until someone is trained to make the decisions.[236] Corresponding with Paul's way of caring new converts, the Korean Presbyterian missionaries in central and southern Philippines share the same partnering attitude. Partnering responsibility for the new churches seems one of the factors that guide missionaries to prefer lifetime commitment to missions.[237]

---

[233] See Table 14 in Chapter Two.

[234] See Table 28 in Chapter Two.

[235] See Table 24 in Chapter Two.

[236] See Table 14 and 28 in Chapter Two.

[237] See Table 17 in Chapter Two.

Willingness to Cooperate

Team spirit is one of the most important strategies in Paul's missions efforts and in all missions work throughout church history. Cooperation with other missionaries, national leaders, and supporting churches is the main concern of this section.

In Paul's ministry, working with others from the beginning to end is a priority. Paul is not a lone ranger, but a leader of a team. He launches his first missions journey with co-missionaries, Barnabas and John. In his second missions journey, Paul works together with Silas, Timothy, Luke, and many others. He chooses elders from the local church and entrusts the new congregations to them. He also maintains a good relationship with his sending churches, and reports his ministries to the Antioch church and the church in Jerusalem..

Survey results show that 90.3% of the respondents claim that cooperation with other missionaries is effective or very effective.[238] The fact that they would plant churches where there is no evangelical church indicates that they accept other evangelical churches. This rules out any intention of competing with existing churches.[239] Their willingness to cooperate with other evangelical churches is noticeable. Sixty-three percent of the respondents declare that they work together with other missionaries. Among them 26.7% claim they would cooperate with others in all their ministries, while 20% affirm that they would cooperate in more than 70% of their ministries, and 16.6% note their cooperation in half of the time with others with the other half work individually.[240]

In cooperation with the national leaders, 38.6% of the respondents cooperate in half of their ministry, excluding finances at least, while 28.95% claim they include financial matters. The rest of the missionaries state that they cooperate with national leaders, but the quality and quantity of cooperation depends on the conditions.[241] Cooperation with the supporting church is low. Thirty-eight point seven percent of the respondents claim that their supporting churches understand their ministries fully, and 25.8% stress that their supporting churches participate in their ministries fully.

In sum, it is clear that the missionary respondents desire to cooperate with other denominational churches, missionaries, national pastoral leaders, and supporting

---

[238]See Table 25 in Chapter Two.

[239]See Table 9 in Chapter Two.

[240]See Table 29 in Chapter Two.

[241]See Table 28 in Chapter Two.

churches. Corresponding with the biblical example, the will to cooperate with others is perceived as a strength of the missions strategies of the respondents.

Endeavor to Adopt Local Cultures

The Korean Presbyterian missionaries in central and southern Philippines move from a monoculture to diverse cultures when they go to the missions field. The diverse culture is one of the greatest obstacles in the advance of their ministries. This calls for contextualzation on the part of the missionaries.

Paul seems to practice contextualization almost unconsciously.[242] Since he was born in a Hellenistic Jewish home in a Gentile environment and received education in Jerusalem, Paul straddles between the Jewish and Gentile cultures. His command of the major languages of the Greco-Roman society is excellent. He strives to make his messages understandable. Unlike the Jewish tradition, Paul mobilizes women in to his attempt to expediting the training of local leaders.

Corresponding with the Pauline foundational principle of contextualization, the missionaries endeavor to learn the local languages, e.g., English, Cebuano, Ilongo, and Tagalog.[243] Since Korea is a monolingual society, Koreans face difficulties in learning other languages. The missionaries, however, claim that they use English and Cebuano as the languages with which they communicate with people. This indicates that the missionsries spend much of their time and energy in learning languages.

Another indication of these missionaries' endeavor to adapt to the local culture is to observe the church anniversary, which is very common in the Philippines.[244] In the field survey, 87% of the respondents claim that they observe church anniversaries. In fact, observing the church anniversary is not common in the Korean church as does the celebration of personal birthdays.[245] However, the majority of the respondents adopt

---

[242]The researcher echoes Tereso C. Casiño's definition of contextualization. Thus: "Contextualization is the dynamic process of appropriating biblical truth within the historical, sociopolitical, economic, religious, and cultural context of a given people, using both contemporary and traditional symbols, speech forms, and paradigms" ("Preaching Workshop in Bible Exposition" [Lecture given at the Visayan Nazarene Bible College chapel in Cebu City, Philippines on February 6, 2001], Library of Cebu Bible College, Cebu City, Philippines).

[243]See Table 30 in Chapter Two.

[244]See Table 33 in Chapter Two.

[245]Koreans do not celebrate personal birthdays in a lavished fashion, except during the first and sixtieth birthdays. When infant mortality was high, Korean people celebrated the first birthday greatly because it indicates the baby as healthy and the chance of life for the baby is high. The sixtieth birthday is regarded as the beginning of one's second life cycle, which is celebrated meaningfully. The rests are routine.

the celebration of church anniversary and birthdays as a positive sign toward contextualization.

Next is the respondents' positive attitude towards mobilizing women for leadership in the local churches. The field survey shows 84% of these missionaries register their support for women leadership as most Filipino churches do.[246]

In sum, corresponding with Paul's foundational principle of contextualization, the field survey presents efforts on the part of respondents to adapt to the local cultures. Although mobilizing women leadership in the church is not fully accepted yet, the respondents show high interest in this matter.

Areas of Weakness

In the past ten years the Korean Presbyterian missionaries in central and southern Philippines achieved great results as discussed in the previous chapter. They, however, made some mistakes in the process. This section will identify and analyze the seven areas of weakness perceived in missions strategies as employed by the respondents.

Table 37. Weaknesses of missions strategies

- Language Acquisition and Competence
- Contextualization (Stereotyped Ministry)
- Understanding Filipino Value System
- Handling Missions Funds
- Establishing Self-Supporting Ministries
- Inadequate Information
- Team Spirit

Weak in Language Acquisition and Competence

---

[246]See Table 16 in Chapter Two.

One area of weaknesses for the Korean Presbyterian missionaries in central and southern Philippines in their missions is non-fluency in the local languages, i.e., English, Cebuano, Ilongo, or Tagalog. Obviously the language problem relates to all other missionary problems.

Paul seems to excel in all the major languages of the Greco-Roman society in his time. Scholars note his competence in Aramaic, Hebrew, Greek, Latin, among others.[247] Because of his ability to speak a good number of local languages, Paul communicates with people from all walls of life. His fluency in language contributes to his success in missionary work.

Unlike the Pauline foundational principles demonstrated in Chapter one, the field survey shows how the Korean Presbyterian missionaries in central and southern Philippines are not enthusiastic in preaching the gospel in the open plaza, and in approaching high-class people of economic-social level. This problem lies in their poor command in the local language.[248]

For equipping leaders, "apprenticeship by missionary" and "correspondence course" are advisable because of transportation and communication problems which are caused by geographical distances. These items mark low in rank because of these missionaries' inadequate facility in language.[249] Although these missionaries declare they employ English, Cebuano, and other local languages as major medium for communication, their fluency seems weak.[250] Thus, inadequate ability in English and other adequate local language is one weakness of the Korean Presbyterian missionaries in central and southern Philippines.

Weak in Contextualization (Stereotyped Ministry)

The task to make the Christianity acceptable to different people in different cultures is complicated. Contextualization is so intricate and dynamic, and there are not ready-made answers to do this. Missionaries have to continually work on how to contextualize the gospel and the church.

In his ministry, Paul rejects an attempt to transplant Judaic practices like

---

[247] Robert L. Reymond, *Paul: A Survey of His Missionary Labors and Theology* (Ross-Shire, Great Britain: Christian Focus Publications, 2000), 47. See also page 65 in Chap One.

[248] See Tables 6 and 8 in Chapter Two.

[249] See Table 13 in Chapter Two.

[250] See Table 30 in Chapter Two.

circumcision, keeping seasons, and fussing over foods in the newly planted churches. For Paul, those practices are non-essentials of the gospel, so that new converts in other cultures do not necessarily need to follow the said Jewish elements. He baptizes new converts immediately after their confession of faith. He starts his preaching in the place where his audiences are as well as uses local illustrations for making his message understandable. He recognizes the efforts of women in his ministries.

In contrast with Pauline principles, field survey shows weaknesses in the practices of ministries among the Korean Presbyterian missionaries in central and southern Philippines. Unlike Paul, some missionaries include non-essential elements in their ministries, namely, "dawn prayer meeting," "Friday vigil prayer meeting," "fasting prayer meeting," "Sunday evening commitment service," and "simultaneous prayer in loud voice."[251] These activities are uncommon in the Filipino churches.

Other uncommon practices include "new year worship service (even if it is not on Sunday)," "children's Sunday service in May," "barley (wheat) harvest thanksgiving service," "Christmas eve service," "Christmas-day service," and "last night of the year service."[252] These activities are generally not observed in the Filipino churches. However, the Korean Presbyterian missionaries in central and southern Philippines unconsciously practice these activities in the Philippines just like their sending churches.

Ninety-four percent of the respondents observe "Thanksgiving Sunday" once a year in November, and 6% of them observe it twice a year (in June and November).[253] June and November, however, are not harvest seasons; rather it is rice-planting season in central and southern Philippines. Furthermore, "Thanksgiving Sunday" in June is inappropriate in the Philippines because it originates from the barley and wheat harvest celebration. Those agricultural crops are not cultivated in the Philippines.[254]

In their preaching ministry, 62% of the respondents seldom use Filipino illustrations in their message for understandability.[255] If these missionaries use unfamiliar sources in their sermons or teaching, their message would be foreign to their audience.

---

[251]See Table 34 in Chapter Two.

[252]See Table 33 in Chapter Two.

[253]See Table 32 in Chapter Two.

[254]Barley and wheat grow only in the place where there is winter season. In Korea, farmers sow a field with barley and wheat after the harvest of rice and before winter season comes, around November. Barley and wheat grow until the temperature drops below zero degrees Celsius. During winter, barley and wheat cease to grow, but they resume to grow from early spring and become ripe in June, just before the season of planting rice. See also Lavoy I. Croy, "Wheat," in *The World Book Encyclopedia*.

[255]See Table 35 in Chapter Two.

Thirty-nine percent of the respondents support utilizing women leadership, including ordination and senior leadership in their churches, while 61% prefer to mobilize women labors, excluding ordination and senior leadership.[256] Also the survey shows a high tendency for the missionaries to set up a Korean-style ministry. In a leadership training program, these missionaries prefer the traditional style of Bible school or seminary, which, for various reasons, is not always desirable to meet the needs of nationals.[257] As examined in the previous chapter, these missionaries prefer the traditional style of training as it is the popular type of training church leaders in their home country. The fact that around 90% of the respondents claim that they emphasize "Korean style" ministries often or seldom in their ministries indicates a serious ministry challenges.[258]

Weak in Understanding the Filipino Value System

Understanding the value system of the people is significant in missionary life because real communication occurs when both parties have the same comprehension of the value system of their community. Misunderstanding the value system could cause serious miscommunication between a missionary and the local people.

Paul's speech indicates his knowledge of the audiences' hidden factors of behaviors, religious backgrounds, and worldviews. Because Paul grew up in a Hellenistic Judaic environment, he understands both Hellenism and Judaism, and he knows how to apply these two different value systems to different people. When he enters a Jewish synagogue, Paul begins his preaching from Jewish history. When he encounters Gentiles, he speaks about pagan gods, which control all their social behaviors. Clearly, understanding the value system is one factor of Paul's success in missions work.

The field survey, however, shows the missionary respondents are weak in this area. One of the most important and often mentioned Filipino values is *"hiya"* which is neglected by foreigners. As examined in previous chapters, if a missionary demands his or her audiences to make a decision to accept Jesus as their personal savior or to receive baptism right away, people would feel *"hiya"* and when they do, it becomes hard to expect real evangelistic fruit. The survey, unfortunately, shows that 74% of the respondents strongly or mildly demand their audience to make a decision.[259]

---

[256]See Table 16 in Chapter Two.

[257]See Table 13 in Chapter Two.

[258]See Table 31 in Chapter Two.

The survey shows that Korean Confucian value system influences the ministries of the missionaries negatively. In traditional Confucian value system in Korea, women do not publicly have a voice. This value seems to have influenced 61 % of respondents to take a somewhat negative attitude in utilizing women labors in the church[260]

Therefore, these missionaries have a weakness in understanding the Filipino value system. Another weakness is the unconscious attempt to practice their innate Korean value system in the Filipino church settings.

Weak in Handling Missions Funds

One of the greatest human social problems is how to handle financial resources properly. To handle missions funds requires great care because it is one of the most vulnerable areas of Satanic assault.

Paul transacts necessary amount of funds in his ministries. He supports himself and his team by making money from his vocation in the market. He is involved in transacting funds, and he, however, let other team member manage the missions funds.

Contrary to the Pauline foundational principles, the survey shows that some missionaries seem to use their missions funds improperly or undesirably. The priority of their missions funds allocation is as follows: (1) co-workers' salary, (2) operating institutions, (3) building construction, (4) rental of property, and (5) evangelism and equipping ministry.[261] It indicates that the missionaries spend most of their missions funds for indirect evangelism. One may criticize it as an unhealthy use of missions funds. Despite the fact that 65% of the missionary respondents claim self-support principle is effective, the fact that they give the first priority to a co-workers' salary in using missions funds is unclear.[262]

In making decision, around 70% of the missionaries do not share equal authority with their national co-workers is discussed in previous chapter.[263] Though ideas of

---

[259] See Table 12 in Chapter Two.

[260] See Table 16 in Chapter Two. The traditional Confucianism in Korea teaches that a woman must follow three men in her whole life. The first man whom she expects to obey is her father until she marries. The second man is her husband after she marries him. The third man is her son when she gets old and her husband dies ahead of her.

[261] See Table 23 in Chapter Two.

[262] See Table 21 in Chapter Two.

national leaders are not always relevant for all situations, it is also undesirable that missionaries alone make all the decisions without national leaders participation. Another negative factor in this area is the influences of the supporting church in Korea.

In sum, the Korean Presbyterian missionaries in central and southern Philippines show a weakness in handling missions funds. Self-supporting missionaries and churches are ideal, but the actual situation is different. National leaders need to share equally with the missionaries in financial matters.

Weak in Establishing Self-Governing Ministries

No missionary is absolutely isolated. Missions work relates closely to the supporting church. The close relationship between the missionary and the supporting church enhances the missions work, but it also has the capability to hinder ministries.

Paul receives no regular financial support from the churches in Jerusalem or in Antioch. This fact could make him work freely without any interference from supporting churches. If he receives regular support from the Jerusalem church, Paul may have difficulties to reject the influences of the Judaic legalism in the Antioch church when he disputes legalism concerning circumcision with the false teachers from Jerusalem (15:1-2). There might be also a possibility that the resolution of the Jerusalem Council would be different.

The field survey, however, shows that the missionaries experience some negative effect caused by the supporting church's unavoidable influences in their ministries. One of the reasons why the missionaries prefer to work with the lower social economic level of people is because of the supporting church's dissatisfaction if these missionaries work with the upper class. Korean Christians have a concept that missionaries should be contented with honest poverty.[264] Why missionaries implement this "Korean style" of activity and observe occasions that are irrelevant to the Filipino church setting may be understood in the same sense.[265] One factor could be the weak volition of the national leaders and missionaries for self-governing church.

Consequently, the missionaries are negatively influenced by their supporting churches in Korea. If supporting churches understand the social cultural background of

---

[263] See Table 28 in Chapter Two.

[264] See Table 8 in Chapter Two. One typical example that Korean supporting churches criticize is the practice of some missionaries to hire a domestic helper, which is common even among poor families in the Philippines. Korean churches, however, have a tendency to understand it as a luxurious life style.

[265] See Tables 31, 32, 33, and 34 in Chapter Two

the missions field, these missionaries would be more effective in ministering to nationals.

Weak in Sufficient Information

In the twenty-first century society, one who holds information will control the world. It is also important for missionaries to have information concerning social, political, economical, cultural, and other religious movement because all of these factors affect, hinder, or enhance missionary work. Furthermore, it is necessary for missionaries to know modern trends in missions in the world church.

In his ministry, Paul has pre-knowledge of the sociopolitical, cultural, geographical, religious structure, government system, court system, Jewish social structure, and others. He has information about the church in Rome before he visits them and has friends in Rome. He organizes his team with members from different areas thus: Barnabas and John from Cyprus, Silas from Jerusalem, Timothy from Lystra, Luke from Macedonia, Aquila and Priscila from Pontus and Italy, and Apollos from Alexandria. All these cultural backgrounds help Paul in missions work. He seems to have inside information in the Roman government and in the Sanhedrin. From these resources Paul obtains information that there is a plot to kill him (19:20; 23:12-16; 25:3).

The field survey shows that only 6.5% of the respondents are working with Muslims, while 84% of them are planting churches and 45% are teaching in theological institutions.[266] One of the reasons why only a few of them concentrate their ministries on tribal people or in tribal areas is the lack of information or access to false information.[267]

In leadership training programs, the survey shows that the missionaries prefer traditional theological institutions.[268] One of the reasons why these missionaries do not use these other programs is the lack of vital information. Other countries use a variety of programs as an alternative strategy.

One of the modern trends in missions is the short-term movement. The field survey, however, shows that 78% of the respondents believe short-term missionaries are not feasible in the missions field.[269] Thus, it is natural for these missionaries to

---

[266]See Table 4 in Chapter Two.

[267]See Table 7 in Chapter Two.

[268]See Table 13 in Chapter Two.

prefer lifetime service on the missions field.[270] Western missiologists, however, have warned about the coming of the short-term wave from early 1990s, and have considered how to effectively use short-term missionaries. One of their ideas is to reap long-term rewards from short-term investments.[271]

In sum, the field survey shows that the Korean Presbyterian missionaries in central and southern Philippines have insufficient information. It is, therefore, necessary for these missionaries and their Korean support church to develop ways to gain proper information and supply it to missionaries. Short-term missions strategies is another area that needs to be developed.

Weak in Team Spirit

Cooperation with missionaries, national leaders, and supporting churches is crucial to the success of missions work.[272] Though the majority of the missionaries claim their ability to cooperate is effective, the reality is that most of them do not work together in their ministries.

Paul is not a lone missionary like Peter and Philip, but a leader member of his missions team. When he is alone in Athens, he asks his team members to join him as soon as possible. He never strives to work alone.

In contrast to Paul's foundational principle of missions strategies, the field survey shows that the cooperative work of the missionary respondents appears inadequate. Fifty percent of these missionaries work with other missionaries cooperatively, but 50 % work alone.[273] Missionaries work generally alone in the church-planting ministry, as

---

[269] See Table 26 in Chapter Two. Paul Borthwick notes positive and negative points for short-term missions. The positive is that cross-cultural opportunities for youth are more available than ever and short-term service develops global citizens and world Christians. The negative is that it may become almost like taking the short-termers to Disneyland. Nevertheless, Borthwick writes that short-term missions are an essential part of the church's role in producing global and missions mined Christians ("Short-term Youth Team: Are They Worth It?" *Evangelical Missions Quarterly* 32 [October 1996], 402-3).

[270] See Table 17 in Chapter Two.

[271] See Footnote 55 in Chapter Two

[272] A survey concludes that career missionaries prefer individual assignments that provide one-on-one relationships with other missionaries, while young missionary candidates between the ages of eighteen and twenty-two favor team assignments. Team assignment seems a trend in missions work (Arnell Motz, "What Generation Xers Think about Mission Teams" *Evangelical Missions Quarterly* 32 [October 1996], 409).

[273] See Table 27 in Chapter Two.

well as cooperate in other ministries such as medical, theological education, equipping, or youth ministry.

The respondents seem to consider "team spirit" as a secondary qualification for being a church leader. The field survey shows the item on "team sprit" ranked fourth.[274] One of the reasons why the missionaries see cooperation as less important lies in the independent character of Korean people. The researcher agrees with other senior missionaries who observe that there is a strong tendency among Korean missionaries not to listen to the advice of those with ministry experiences.[275] Because of their strong independent character, team spirit appears unimportant. The strong independent personality causes a lose connection between themselves and it may create a weak team spirit. The ineffective structure of missions agency seems to be one other reason.

The Confucian philosophy in Korea that says an older or higher poisoned person is wiser and would not be questioned may become another reason. This concept may stimulate the pastor of a supporting church to control the missionary and missions strategies. Consequently, there is seldom a high quality of cooperation between missionaries and national leaders.

Another area that needs to be improved is in the cooperation between missionaries and their supporting churches. Fifty-one point six percent of the respondents claim that supporting churches need to understand missions, and 10 % admit no assurance of cooperation.[276] In this situation, full cooperation in missions is difficult.

In sum, the Korean Presbyterian missionaries in central and southern Philippines lack team spirit. Cooperation among missionaries, between the missionaries and the national coworker, and the missionaries and the supporting churches is therefore insufficient.

Summary of the Chapter

This chapter sought to identify and analyze the strengths and weaknesses of

---

[274]See Table 15 in Chapter Two.

[275]Koreans used self-scorn saying, "Koreans are like the gravel, not like the clay; Individuals are good, but cooperation is impossible."

[276]See Table 29 in Chapter Two.

missions strategies employed by the Korean Presbyterian missionaries in central and southern Philippines. There were seven areas of strength and weakness discussed in this chapter.

The first section of this chapter identified major strengths of missions strategies employed by the Korean Presbyterian missionaries in central and southern Philippines. Most of these missionaries showed a high level of zeal for evangelism. Because of their eagerness for winning souls, the statistics of their achievement is higher than the nation as a whole. Spiritual sensitivity is another perceived strength of these missionaries. Accordingly, these missionaries are sensitive to the guidance of the Holy Spirit in their ministries. Next is their strong identity to hold fast to the Calvinistic reformed tradition and theology. The missionaries would pay much attention to the equipping of national leaders, which resulted in the establishment of four theological institutions in each major missions station. They also tried to turn over the leadership of the church to national leaders. Partnership responsibility is another aspect of the missionaries' strength. Acting as partner, they would take care of their churches with passion and love. They would help churches until the latter become self-supporting. Missionary respondents also would cooperate with other Great Commission Christians and leaders. Survey showed how they try to adopt to local cultures, and to adjust and identify with their national counterparts.

The other section of this chapter identified areas of weakness in the missions strategies employed by the Korean Presbyterian missionaries in central and southern Philippines. The first relates to barrier in language. Since Korean missionaries came from a mono-lingual country, it is difficult for many of them to acquire another language as an adult. One of the greatest problems missionaries face is in the area of contextualization. In many ways, these missionaries attempted to transplant Korean churches in central and southern Philippines, which resulted in conflict with local cultures. Their stereotyped ministry became an obstacle for the advancement of the local church. Noted, too, was need for missionaries to invest more time in studying Filipino value systems, which underlay Filipino behavior. Research showed how the improper use of missions funds could cause problem among missionaries. Along with this was the extreme influence on missions work exerted by supporting churches in Korea. Towards the end of the chapter, the researcher discussed how inadequate cooperation among missionaries, national leaders, and the supporting churches could hinder the effectiveness of missions work of the Korean Presbyterian missionaries in central and southern Philippines.

Conclusion

This concluding section is divided into two parts: a summary of the findings of the research sub-problems, and the implications of this dissertation's findings.

Summary

This study investigated the missions strategies that Korean Presbyterian missionaries in central and southern Philippines employed in their missionary work between 1990 and 2000. In conducting this research the following problem was explored: "What are the strengths and weaknesses of the missions strategies of the Korean Presbyterian missionaries in central and southern Philippines in the light of Paul's missions strategies in Acts 13-28?" In response to this problem, three sub-problems were examined with the use of literary research and field survey.

Chapter One dealt with the following sub-problem: "What are Paul's missions strategies evident in Acts 13-28?" In dealing with this sub-problem prior to conducting this study, the researcher assumed that Paul employed missions strategies which could be ascertained in Acts 13-28. The researcher chose Paul's six missions strategies as endorsed by biblical and missions scholars: (1) strategies in planting church, (2) strategies in preaching the gospel, (3) strategies in equipping leaders, (4) strategies in financing ministries, (5) strategies in team ministries, and (6) strategies in contextualized communications.

The first chapter surveyed Paul's missions strategies in Acts 13-28 as the fundamental principles for all missions work down through history. It was assumed that these strategies are crucial to missionary tasks. In planting churches, Paul would choose a strategic location, select receptive people, and employ effective methods. Accordingly, Paul understood the socio-political situations, cultures, and the geography of the Roman Empire. The study showed how Paul would discern a strategic location, looked for responsive people, and utilized creative methods in church planting ministries.

Paul's life and ministry indicated a clear understanding of his tasks, which he received from God. This determined the content of his message, i.e., Jesus Christ. The starting point of Paul's preaching varied according to his audience and circumstances, but the heart of his message was always Jesus Christ. Evidently, he took a stern stance towards all non-Christian religions and refused to compromise with them. He would approach people of other religions with care and tact. This section also discussed the characteristics of Paul's message as follows: clarity, persuasiveness, urgency, Scripture oriented, and contextualization.

Research pointed out Paul's emphasis on the importance of local leadership in the church. In installing local leadership in the church, Paul would choose local leaders, following the guidance of the Holy Spirit. The Holy Spirit initiates and expedites Paul's missionary work. Paul creatively mobilized women leadership in his missions work. He would establish local leadership on the basis of doctrinal, practical, and spiritualfoundations. The methods Paul utilized for local leadership training program were also examined in this chapter. In his missions work and management of missions teams, Paul needed a strong financial base. However, his ministries did not depend on financial support. Instead, he introduced the twin concepts "self-supporting missionary" and "self-supporting church. Research showed Paul's stress on the use of "missionary team" and "team ministry" as effective missions strategies. As a team leader, Paul showed how to work effectively with other members of the team.

The chapter also established how Paul managed to take advantage of his background as a Hellenistic Jew for the sake of missions. Educated in Jerusalem, his ministry extended beyond the geographical and cultural boundaries of Judea. In his missionary journeys, Paul made significant efforts to make his message relevant to the local context. He would contextualize his message in each culture, using symbols and methods that appropriate to people from with Jewish and Greek backgrounds. Paul understood the need for paradigm change and shifts when confronted by rigid monotheists, polytheists, and pantheists of his time.

Chapter Two dealt with the following sub-problem: "What are the missions strategies of the Korean Presbyterian missionaries in central and southern Philippines from 1990 to 2000?" Before conducting field survey, the researcher assumed that there were identifiable missions strategies of the Korean Presbyterian missionaries in central and southern Philippines. The survey was conducted in two parts. The first part presented basic information about the missionaries and their work. This included a brief history and the missions work of the four missions groups of the Korean Presbyterian Church, and an analysis of the general information of the missionaries. A brief history on the history and work of the following Korean Presbyterian missions groups was given: KPCK, KPCH, KPCT, and KPCKH. Attention was given to the history involving pioneering missionaries as it shed light on how the missionary work progressed since its inception. The section presented the general information of the missionaries' ministerial status, age range, and length of time in missions work. An analysis of ministries and church growth followed the general information. This part presented the present status of missions work and the numerical growth of the churches and baptized members, plus the number of national workers, and the missionaries from 1990 to 2000. Field survey showed that the church grew slowly from 1990 to 1994, and then grew rapidly from 1995 as missionaries gained more experiences, along with the emergence of national workers in planting new churches.

The second part showed missions strategies, which included planting church, preaching the gospel, equipping leaders, financing ministry, team ministry, and contextualized communication. Here, a detailed statistical analysis was presented, which followed the outline used in Chapter One for the sake of correlation. Results of the field survey were analyzed, and the respondents' responses were interpreted according to appropriate statistical tools.

Chapter Three dealt with the following sub-problem, "What are the strengths and weaknesses of the Korean Presbyterian missionaries in central and southern Philippines from 1990 to 2000?" Prior to conducting the study, the researcher assumed that there were strengths and weaknesses in the missions strategies employed by the Korean Presbyterian missionaries in central and southern Philippines, in relation to Paul's missions strategies and to the growth of the church on which these missionaries have worked. The researcher noticed seven strengths and seven weaknesses.

The chapter noted that most Korean Presbyterian missionaries in central and southern Philippines demonstrated a high level of evangelistic fervor, which correlated with Paul's emphasis on sharing the gospel in different areas. Spiritual sensitivity ranked high as a perceived strength among the missionaries. Another noted strength was "theological identity," in this case, Presbyterian or Calvinistic Reformed theology, which the missionaries held on to. The fact that Korean ministers dislike changing their denominational affiliation contributed to church growth in central and southern Philippines. Most of the missionaries normally cooperated with national church leaders. This desire for cooperation drove them to establish equipping ministries. The persistence to equip national leaders provided missionaries a strong foundation in their missions task. Missionaries also had the willingness to transfer the leadership to local leaders. In doing so, they maintain strong connections with newly planted churches and practiced good ministry stewardship. Newly planted churches were not left to fend for themselves, but rather developed into self-sufficient communities as early as possible. The complexities of working among different cultures and sub-cultures did not hinder the missionaries' zeal to work closely with the local people. This allowed them to adopt the local culture as a basic strategy in missionary work.

On the other hand, research showed the weaknesses in the missions strategies of the Korean missionaries in central and southern Philippines. The first weakness concerned with language barrier. This was complicated by the fact that Korean missionaries did not only have to learn English but also the local dialects, which people use in their daily lives. Next to language problem was the failure to contextualize ministries. Survey showed how most Korean Presbyterian missionaries in central and southern Philippines thought of ministry forms and practices as universal. So, they ended up transporting Korean-oriented ministries, which did not fit the Filipino church setting. This was evident by their lack of understanding the Filipino cultural value systems. Noted, too, was the weakness in handling finances in the missions field. Survey indicated that most Korean Presbyterian missionaries in central and southern Philippines tended to control missions funds and refuse to share control with their national co-workers. Another weakness noted was the influence of the supporting church in Korea, as sending churches did not have much understanding about the missions field. Survey revealed that supporting churches would withhold financial resources, which limited the ability of missionaries to work independently and creatively. Then, there was the noticeable lack of information about the trends in world missions and other socio-political aspects that affected missions work in the Philippines. Towards the end of the chapter, discussion centered on the weakness of the lack of teamwork amongKorean missionaries themselves, between missionaries and Filipino workers, and between missionaries and their supporting bodies in Korea.

Implications of the Findings

In the light of the above conclusions, the following implications seem appropriate:

1. There is a need for Korean missionaries to acknowledge the necessity of overcoming the language barriers and to improve their language acquisition skills. Sufficient time and resources need to be given to both missionaries-in-training and career missionaries in the Philippines

2. Korean missionaries need to be exposed in various aspects of cross-cultural missions settings prior to their deployment. To surmount a narrow-minded worldview caused by mono-language, mono-race, and mono-culture society , a multi-cultural training setting under a qualified mentor, both in Korea and in the Philippines is recommended.

3. The lack of understanding the Filipino society calls for Korean missionaries to study the value systems and the socio-economic, religious, and political traditions of the Philippines. The missionaries need to have an in-depth anthropological knowledge of the Filipino people.

4. There is a need to develop some alternative plans for the arrangement of missions funds. The practices of these missionaries controlling missions funds alone need to be reconsidered. Financial principles need to be clear to all the participants, missionaries, national leaders, and supporting churches.

5. Missionary sending bodies need to trust and support the missions strategies that their missionaries have formulated according to the needs and cultural environments of the Filipinos.

6. Sufficient information of modern missions trend and other socio-political information, both international and local, are compulsory for Korean missionaries. Thus, supporting churches and missions agencies need to supply information by sending newspapers, magazines, journals, and other materials. For prompt supply of information, networking of qualified and competent persons in these trends need to be encouraged.

7. In the light of the Korean Presbyterian missionaries' pattern of working independently, team spirit need to be developed. This requires Korean missionaries to avoid duplicate investments of missions resources. This may call for the formation of a trans-denominational team or council that could provide extensive information to missionaries with regard to the use of resources in various areas.

8. To meet the increased need of highly educated missionaries or professionals especially in the area of theological education, new missionaries need to take higher degrees prior to their deployment. Career missionaries need to be encouraged to use their furlough for additional training and education.

9. Alongside formal theological education in the missions field, missionaries need non-formal discipleship formation exposures in various situations. There is thus a need for Korean missionaries to receive training on how to make disciples in multi-cultural settings.

10. The fact that majority of the Korean missionaries work in urbanized areas means the lack of church planters among ethno-linguistic groups and Muslims. This calls for new strategies in doing missions work among the ethno-linguistic groups and the Muslims in central and southern Philippines.

APPENDIX A

LETTER TO THE CHAIRPERSON OF A MISSION GROUP

Date

Dear Sir:

Greetings in Christ's name!

I am a student at the Asia Baptist Graduate Theological Seminary in Baguio City, Philippines. At present, I am working on a dissertation entitled, "An Analysis of the Missions Strategies of the Korean Presbyterian Missionaries in Central and Southern Philippines in the Light of Paul's Missions Strategies." This is part of my requirements for the Doctor of Theology degree at ABGTS.

Important parts of this dissertation are insights from missionaries assigned in central and southern Philippines who currently work under your leadership. All data and information from these missionaries will be valuable to my study and the future ministries of others in the Philippines. The purpose of this study is to seek a way to improve the ministries of the missionaries in this region by determining the strengths and weaknesses of the missions strategies of the Korean Presbyterian missionaries in the light of Paul's missions strategies.

Thus, I would like to request your good office to endorse the sending and gathering of the questionnaire attached herein. I will greatly appreciate your assistance.

Sincerely yours,

Hoo-Soo Nam

APPENDIX B

LETTER TO KOREAN PRESBYTERIAN MISSIONARIES IN CENTRAL AND SOUTHERN PHILIPPINES

Date

Greetings in Christ's name!

I am a student at the Asia Baptist Graduate Theological Seminary in Baguio City, Philippines. At present, I am working on a dissertation entitled, "An Analysis of the Missions Strategies of the Korean Presbyterian Missionaries in Central and Southern Philippines in the Light of Paul's Missions Strategies." This is part of my requirements for the Doctor of Theology degree at ABGTS.

Important parts of this dissertation would come from the missionaries serving in this region. All data and information from you will be valuable to my study and the future ministries of all others in this region. The purpose of this study is to seek a way to improve our ministries by determining the strengths and weaknesses of the missions strategies of the Korean Presbyterian Missionaries in the light of Paul's missions strategies.

Thus, I would like to request you to answer the enclosed questionnaire. Please read the questions carefully and fill them out according to the instructions. Please return the filled out questionnaire as soon as possible using a self-addressed, stamped envelope enclosed. I greatly appreciate your cooperation.

Sincerely yours,

Hoo-Soo Nam

APPENDIX C

MISSIONS STATIONS OF THE KOREAN PRESBYTERIAN MISSIONARIES IN CENTRAL AND SOUTHERN PHILIPPINES

☐ Missions stations (Cebu, Davao, Dumaguete, Iloilo)

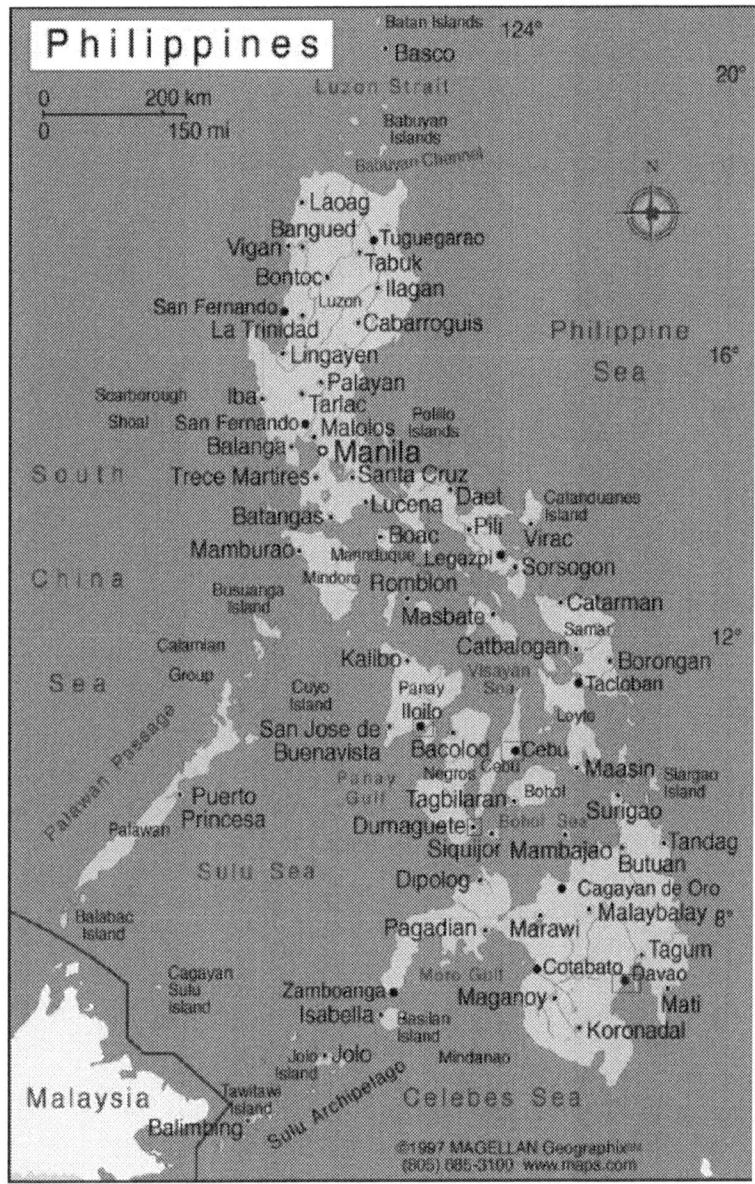

APPENDIX D

A SURVEY QUESTIONNAIRE FOR THE KOREAN PRESBYTERIAN MISSIONARIES IN CENTRAL AND SOUTHERN PHILIPPINES

I. General Profile

1. Name of Missions Organization:

2. How long have you been involved in missionary service?

3. Age:

4. Educational Achievement:

   ( )High-School
   ( )College
   ( )Graduate school-M.Div., M.A., and others ( )
   ( )Graduate school-Th.M and above

5. Ministry Status:

   ( ) Ordained, ( ) Licensed, ( ) Missionary wife, ( ) Lay-missionary

II. Questions

1. What do you think are the most effective strategies for the early stages of church planting? (Please check all possible answers and rank by order of importance with 1 being the most important and 7 being the least.)

   ( ) Personal evangelism
   ( ) House worship
   ( ) Home Bible study
   ( ) Contact community leaders first (e.g., Mayor, Barangay Captain, Council members)
   ( ) Proclaim the gospel in the open plaza
   ( ) Debate with other religious scholars
   ( ) Contact religious leaders of the community first

2. What region do you think is the most strategic place for planting a church? (Please check all possible answers and rank by order of importance with 1 being the most important and 5 being the least.)

( ) City (Urban area)
( ) Municipal town (Semi-urban area)
( ) Rural Area – Barrio
( ) Tribal People area
( ) Other (Please specify)

3. What group of people is your target? (Please check all possible answers and rank by order of importance with 1 being the most important and 6 being the least.)

( ) Upper class (in financial income)
( ) Lower class (in financial income)
( ) Professionals
( ) Career group (e.g. factory workers, drivers, etc.)
( ) Farmers/Fishermen
( ) Any people

4. What primary concern do you think a missionary should consider in choosing an area for church planting? (Please check all possible answers and rank by order of importance with 1 being the most important and 5 being the least.)

( ) Good receptivity of the people
( ) Strategic location
( ) Where the Holy Spirit guides
( ) Where no evangelical church is found
( ) Other (Please specify)

5. What type of message do you use most often? (Please check all possible answers and rank by order of importance with 1 being the most important and 5 being the least.)

( ) Presbyterian doctrines and beliefs
( ) Christian ethics
( ) A need-focused message (e.g., healing, blessing, problem solving, etc.)
( ) Christ-centered message (e.g., cross, resurrection, redemption, etc.)
( ) Other (Please specify)

6. What is your attitude toward other religions like Roman Catholic and Islam in your preaching? (Please check one only)

( ) Strongly hostile
( ) Mildly hostile
( ) Neutral
( ) Mildly tolerant
( ) Strongly tolerant

7. How do you conclude your preaching or teaching? (e.g., In accepting Jesus Christ as personal savior, receiving baptism, etc. Please check one only)

   ( ) Strongly demand to make decision
   ( ) Mildly demand to make decision
   ( ) Just invite to make decision
   ( ) No mention of making a decision
   ( ) Other (Please specify)

8. What type of leadership training program do you think is appropriate in your context? (Please check all possible answers and rank by order of importance with 1 being the most important and 7 being the least.)

   ( ) Bible school, seminary
   ( ) Theological Education by Extension
   ( ) Correspondence Course
   ( ) Apprenticeship by missionary
   ( ) Apprenticeship by other persons who learned first
   ( ) Short-term training or seminars
   ( ) Other (Please specify)

9. How long do you think a missionary should hold the leadership of the church? (Please check one only)

   ( ) Until the church elects one elder
   ( ) Until the church can support itself
   ( ) Until a Filipino pastor can lead
   ( ) Until the missionary leaves
   ( ) Other (Please specify)

10. What qualification do you consider when you choose a pastoral leader or a co-worker? (Please check all possible answers and rank by order of importance with 1 being the most important and 8 being the least.)

    ( ) Strong spirituality
    ( ) Gifted and trained for leadership
    ( ) Teachability
    ( ) Calling from God
    ( ) Team spirit
    ( ) Theological Background
    ( ) Faithfulness
    ( ) Other (Please specify)

11. How much do you think the women-leadership should be practiced in the Philippine church setting? (Please check one only)

( ) Always, including ordination for pulpit ministry and senior pastorate
( ) Always, excluding ordination for pulpit ministry and senior pastorate
( ) Occasionally
( ) Never
( ) Not sure

12. How long do you think is the ideal period for a missionary to serve in the missions field? (Please check one only)

    ( ) 1-5 years
    ( ) 5–10 years
    ( ) 10-15 years
    ( ) 15-20 years
    ( ) More than 20 years
    ( ) Life-time

13. What principles should a new missionary need to follow? (Please check all possible answers and rank by order of importance with 1 being the most important and 5 being the least)

    ( ) Waiting until the time when the direct guidance of the Holy Spirit comes
    ( ) Following the guidance of the Holy Spirit through the church
    ( ) Following the guidance of the leaders of the church or missions agency
    ( ) Following the guidance of senior missionaries
    ( ) Following own decision after long consideration

14. What gifts do you think are important for missionaries? (Please check all possible answers and rank by order of importance with 1 being the most important and 8 being the least)

    ( ) Healing power
    ( ) Speaking in tongue
    ( ) Prophecy (preaching or teaching the Bible)
    ( ) Discerning of spirit
    ( ) Faith
    ( ) Ministry (serving people)
    ( ) Exhortation
    ( ) Giving (mercy)

15. What do you think of a national church leader supported by Korean church directly? (Please check one only)

    ( ) Effective
    ( ) Not sure
    ( ) Ineffective

16. How effective do you think is the "self-support" principle in Philippine setting from the beginning of the church? (Please check one only)

   ( ) Effective
   ( ) Not sure
   ( ) Ineffective

17. Regarding financial support, what type of missionary do you think is effective in your setting? (Please check all possible answers and rank by order of importance with 1 being the most important and 7 being the least.)

   ( ) Self-supporting or tent-making
   ( ) Fully supported by sending church including family living allowance and project expenses
   ( ) Fully supported by host church including family living allowance and project expenses
   ( ) Partially supported; family living allowance provided by self-support or tent-making, project expenses by sending church
   ( ) Partially supported; family living allowance by sending church, project expenses by hosting church
   ( ) Partially supported; family living allowance by host church, project expenses by sending church
   ( ) Other (Please specify)

18. Regarding missions funds, where do you use them mainly? (Please check all possible answers and rank by order of importance with 1 being the most important and 9 being the least.)

   ( ) Co-worker's salary
   ( ) Rental (e.g., church, school, etc.)
   ( ) Scholarship for youth (e.g., tuition, transportation, etc.)
   ( ) Building construction (e.g., church, school, etc.)
   ( ) Compassionate ministry (e.g., regular support for squatter area family, feeding, etc.)
   ( ) Evangelism (e.g., gospel tracts, crusade, film showing, supply Bible, etc.)
   ( ) Operating institutions (e.g., kindergarten, elementary, Bible school, seminary, etc.)
   ( ) Equipping ministry (e.g., seminar, conference, youth camp, church officers retreat, etc.)
   ( ) Other (Please specify)

19. How long do you think is it appropriate to support a church financially? (Please check one only)

   ( ) Until it has 50-70 baptized members
   ( ) Until it has 70-100 baptized members

( ) Until it has its own church building and parsonage
( ) Until it can fully support itself
( ) Maximum first 5 years
( ) Maximum first 7 years
( ) Maximum first 10 years
( ) Never from the beginning
( ) Other (Please specify)

20. How effective do you think missionaries work together? (Please check one only)

( ) Very effective
( ) Effective
( ) Not sure
( ) Ineffective
( ) Very ineffective

21. Do you think a short-term Korean missionary (one or two year) can be helpful for your ministry? (Please check one only)

( ) Yes
( ) No
( ) Not sure
( ) Other (Please specify)

22. How much do you work together with other missionaries? (Please check one only)

( ) Cooperation In all ministries
( ) Mostly in cooperation (above 70%)
( ) About 50% of ministries
( ) Mostly individual (above 70%)
( ) No cooperation

23. In making decision, who holds the authority between you and your national co-worker(s)? (Please check one only)

( ) National co-worker(s) including financials
( ) Half and half including financials
( ) Half and Half excluding financials
( ) Flexible according to the situation
( ) Missionary alone

24. How much do you think your supporting churches understand your ministries and participate in it? (Please check one only)

( ) Fully understnad, fully participate
( ) Fully understand, particially participate

( ) Particially understand, Partially participate
( ) Not sure
( ) Minimal understand, minimal participate

25. What language do you use mainly in your ministry? (Please check all possible answers and rank by order of importance with 1 being the most important and 5 being the least.)

( ) English
( ) Cebuano
( ) Ilongo
( ) Tagalog
( ) Other (Please specify)

26. How much do you think a missionary can emphasize "Korean style" in his or her ministry? (Please check one only)

( ) Always
( ) Often
( ) Seldom
( ) Never

27. How often do you observe "Thanksgiving Sunday" in a year? (Please check one only)

( ) Once a year in November or in other month
( ) Twice a year in June and November or other months
( ) Three times a year (Please check the months you observe. Jan., Feb., March, April, May, June, July, Aug., Sept., Oct., Nov., Dec.)
( ) Never

28. What special occasions do you observe in your church? (Please check all that you observe in your church in the Philippines)

( ) New Year Worship Service (even it is not on Sunday)
( ) Good Friday noon service
( ) Easter dawn union worship with other churches at a special place
( ) Children's Sunday service in May
( ) Parent's Sunday service in May
( ) Barley (Wheat) harvest thanksgiving service
( ) Thanksgiving service
( ) Church anniversary service
( ) Christmas Eve service
( ) Christmas-day service
( ) Last night of the year service
( ) Other (Please specify)

29. What activities do you implement in your ministries? (Please check all that you practice in your church)

   ( ) Dawn prayer meeting
   ( ) Friday vigil prayer meeting
   ( ) Fasting prayer meeting
   ( ) Wednesday evening prayer meeting
   ( ) Cell group prayer meeting
   ( ) Revival meeting
   ( ) The whole congregation retreat
   ( ) Sunday evening commitment service
   ( ) The whole member attending Sunday
   ( ) Occasional thanksgiving offering
   ( ) Regular visitation of member's house
   ( ) Sunday evening service
   ( ) Simultaneous prayer in loud voice
   ( ) Tithe
   ( ) Other (Please specify)

30. How often do you use Filipino poems, idioms, issues, stories, legends, epigrams or other literary forms in your sermons or teachings? (Please check one only)

   ( ) Frequently
   ( ) Often
   ( ) Seldom
   ( ) Never

WORKS CITED

Books

Allen, Roland. *Missionary Methods: St. Paul's or Ours?* Grand Rapids, MI: William. B. Eerdmans Publishing Company, 1962.

Andress, Tomas Quintin D., and Pilar Corazon B. Ilada-Andress, *Making Filipino Values Work for You*. Makati, Philippines: St. Paul Publications, 1986.

Barnes, Albert. *Notes on the New Testament: Acts*. Edited by Robert Frew. London: Blackie and Son, 1885. Reprint, Grand Rapids, MI: Baker Books, 1998.

Bavink, J. H. *An Introduction to the Science of Missions*. Trans.D. H. Freeman. Grand Rapids, MI: Baker Book House, 1960.

Beyerhaus, Peter. *Shaken Foundation: Theological Foundations for Mission.* Grand Rapids, MI: Zondervan Publishing House, 1972.

Blauw, J. *The Missionary Nature of the Church*. New York: McGraw Hill, 1962.

Bosch, David J. *Transforming Mission.* Maryknoll, New York: Orbis Books, 1991.

Bristow, John Temple. *What Paul Really Said about Women*. San Francisco, CA: Harper and Row, 1988.

Brock, Charles. *The Principles and Practice of Indigenous Church Planting.* Nashville, TE: Broadman Press, 1981.

Bruce, F. F. *Paul: Apostle of the Heart Set Free.* Grand Rapids, MI: William Eerdmans Publishing Company, 1978.

_____. *New Testament History.* Garden City, NY: Doubleday & Co., Inc., 1971.

_____. *New Testament History*. Translated by Yong-Wha Na. Seoul: Christian Literature Crusade, 1983.

Chaney, Charles L. and Ron S. Lewis. *Design for Church Growth.* Nashvill, TN: Broadman Press, 1977.

Chang, Joseph Jung-Yeol. *Missions And Church Growth.* Seoul: Sung Kwang

Publishing Co., 1978.

Clark, C. A. *The Work of the Pastor.* Seoul: Korea Christian Publishing, 1981.

Cook, Harold R. *Missionary Life and Work.* Chicago: Moody Press, 1959.

Costas, Orlando E. *The Integrity of Mission: The Inner Life and Outreach of the Church.* New York, NY: Harper & Row, 1979.

Dawson, John. *Taking Our Cities for God: How to Break Spiritual Strongholds.* Lake Mary, FL: Creation House, 1989.

Dodd, C. H. *The Apostolic Preaching and Its Developments.* New York: Haper & Brothers, Publishers, 1960.

Dunn, James D. G. *The Theology of Paul the Apostle.* Grand Rapids, MI: William B. Eerdmans Publishing Company, 1998.

Ellingsen, Mark. *The Evangelical Movement.* Minneapolis, MN: Augsburg Publishing House, 1988.

Ellis, E. Earle. *Pauline Theology.* Grand Rapids, MI: William B. Eerdmans Publishing Company, 1989.

Faircloth, Samuel D. *Church Planting for Reproduction.* Grand Rapids, MI: Baker Book House, 1991.

Febre, Francisco A, Jr. *Introduction to Statistics.* Quezon City, Philippines: Phoenix Publishing House, 1987. Reprint, 1997.

Fink, Arlene. *How to Analyze Survey Data.* Thousand Oaks, CA: SAGE Publishing, 1995.

Fox, Robin Lane. *Pagans and Christianity.* New York: Alfred A. Knopf Publisher, 1989.

France, R. T. *Women in the Church's Ministry: A Test-case for Biblical Hermeneutics.* Cumbria, UK: The Paternoster Press, 1995.

Garvie, Alfred Ernest, *The Christian Preacher.* New York: Charles Scribner's Sons, 1928.

Green, Michael. *Evangelism in the Early Church.* Grand Rapids, MI: William B. Eerdmans Publishing Company, 1970.

Guthrie, Donald. *New Testament Introduction.* Box F. Downers Grove, IL: Inter-Varsity

Press, 1970.

Hadaway, C. Kirk Hadaway, Stuart A. Wright, and Francis M. DuBose. *Home Cell Groups and House Churches*, Nashville, TN: Broadman Press, 1987.

Harman, Allan M. *Covenant and Missions*. Pusan, Korea: Kosin University Press, 1999.

Hedlund, Roger E. *The Mission of the Church in the World: A Biblical Theology.* Grand Rapids, MI: Baker Book House, 1985.

Hesselgrave, David J. *Planting Churches Cross-Culturally: A Guide for Home and Foreign Missions.* Grand Rapids, MI: Baker Book House, 1980.

_____. and Edward Rommen. *Contextualization: Meanings, Methods, and Models.* Grand Rapids, MI: Baker Book House, 1989.

Hiebert, Paul G. *Anthropological Insights for Missionaries.* Grand Rapids, MI: Baker Book House, 1985.

Hodges, M. L. *A Guide to Church Planting.* Chicago: Moody Press, 1973.

Hong, Eu-Pyo. *Present-Day Churchly Trends.* Daegu, Seoul: Bo Mun Publishing Co., 1979.

Hwang, Tae-Yun, ed. *Directory of Korean Missions and Missionaries in the Philippines* "1999." Manila, Philippines: The Association of Korean Missions in the Philippines, 1999.

Johnson, Dennis E. *The Massage of Acts in the History of Redemption.* Phillipsburg, NJ: P & R Publishing Company, 1997.

Johnstone, Patrick. *Operation World*. 5th ed. Carlisle, UK: OM Publishing, 1993. Reprint, with corrections, Carlisle, UK: OM Publishing, 1995.

Jun, Ho-Jin. *Missiology.* Seoul: The Korea Society of Reformed Faith and Conduct, 1989.

_____. *Religious Pluralism and Mission Strategy for Other Religions.* Seoul: The Korea Society of Reformed Faith and Conduct, 1992.

Jung, Byung-Kwan, *The Challenges to the Modern Ministry and Missions.* Seoul: The Word of Life Press, 1994.

Kane, J. Herbert. *Christian Missions in Biblical Perspective.* Grand Rapids, MI: Baker Book House, 1976.

____. *Life and Work on the Mission Field.* Grand Rapids, MI: Baker Book House, 1980.

Kim, Geraldo H., ed., *Presbyterian Government.* Quezon City, Philippines: Presbyterian Church of the Philippines, 1995.

Kim, Jae-Yong and Young-Sook Yoon. *The Missionary Work in the Philippines: God's Merciful Hands.* Pusan, Korea: Korea Publishing Company, 1995.

Kim, Jun-Seop. *An Introduction to Philosophy.* Seoul: Bak Young Sa, 1977.

Kraemer, Hendrik. *The Christian Message in a Non-Christian World.* Grand Rapids, MI: Kregel Publications, 1977.

Kraft, Charles H. *Christianity in Culture: A Study in Dynamic Biblical Theologizing in Cross-Cultural Perspective.* Maryknoll, NY: Orbis Books, 1979.

Lancion, Conrado M. Jr. *Fast Facts About Philippine Provinces.* Manila, Philippines: Tahanan Book, 1995.

Lee, Tai-Woong. *The Theory and Practice of Korean Missions.* Seoul: GMF Press, 1994.

Lindsell, Harold. *An Evangelical Theology of Missions.* Grand Rapids, MI: Zondervan Publishing House, 1970.

Lloyd-Jones, D. Martyn. *Preaching and Preachers.* Grand Rapids, MI: Zondervan Publishing House, 1971

Loewenich, Walther. *Paul: His Life and Work.* London: Oliver and Boyd, 1960.

Lupdag, Anselmo. *Educational Psychology.* Quezon City, Philippines: National Book Store, Inc., 1984.

Machen, J. Gresham. *The Literature and History of New Testament Times.* Translated by Hyo-Seong Kim. Seoul: Sung Kwang Publishing Co., 1980.

McGavran, Donald. *The Bridges of God.* New York: Friendship Press, 1955.

Meeks, Wayne A. *The First Urban Christians.* New Heaven: Yale University Press. 1983.

Meyendorff, John. *Witness to the World.* Crestwood, NY: St. Vladimir's Seminary Press, 1987.

Miles, Delos. *Introduction to Evangelism*. Nashville, TN: Broadman Press, 1983.

Miranda-Feliciano, Evelyn. *Filipino Values and Our Christian Faith*. Manila: OMF Literature Inc., 1990.

Min, Kyung-Bae. *Church History of Korea*. Korea: The Christian Literature Society, 1973.

Oriondo, Leonora Loyola, and Eleanor M. Dallo-Antonio. *Evaluation Educational Outcomes (Tests, Measurement and Evaluation)*. Manila: Rex Book Store, 1984.

Pate, Larry. *Starting New Churches*. Brussels: International Correspondence Institute, 1987.

Patte, Daniel. *Paul's Faith and the Power of the Gospel: A Structural Introduction to the Pauline Letters*. Philadelphia: Fortress Press, 1983.

Pentecost, Edward C. *Issues in Missiology: An Introduction* Grand Rapids, MI: Baker Book House, 1982.

Peters, George W. *A Biblical Theology of Missions*. Chicago: Moody Press, 1972.

Reed, Lyman E. *Preparing Missionaries for Intercultural Communication: A Bi-cultural Approach*. Pasadena, CA: William Carey Library, 1985.

Reimer, Ivoni Richter. *Women in the Acts of the Apostles*. Translated by Linda M. Maloney. Minneapolis, MN: Fortress Press, 1995.

Reymond, Robert L. *Paul: A Survey of His Missionary Labors and Theology*. Ross-Shire, Great Britain: Christian Focus Publications, 2000.

Rheenen, Gaily Van. *Communicating Christ in Animistic Context*. Grand Rapids, MI: Baker Book House, 1991.

____. *Missions: Biblical Foundation and Contemporary Strategies*. Grand Rapids, MI: Zondervan Publishing House, 1996.

Richardson, Don. *Peach Child*. Translated by Jichan Kim. Seoul: Word of Life Press, 1987.

Scott, C. A. Anderson. *Christianity According to St. Paul*. London: Cambridge University Press, 1966.

Seamands, John T. *Tell It Well: Communicating the Gospel Across Cultures*. Kansas City, MO: Beacon Hill Press of Kansas City, 1981.

Sneller, Alvin Roy. *Calvinian Theology and Missions*. Seoul: Sung Kwang Press, 1988.

Sweazey, George E. *Preaching the Good News*. Englewood Cliffs, NJ: Prentice-Hall, Inc., 1976.

Tenney, Merrill C. *New Testament Survey*. Grand Rapids, MI: William B. Eerdmans Publishing Co., 1961.

Wagner, C. Peter. *Church Planting for a Greater Harvest*. Ventura, CA: Regal Books, 1990.

____. *Frontiers in Missionary Strategy*. Chicago: Moody Press, 1978.

Weatherspoon, Jesse Burton. *Sent Forth to Preach*. New York: Harper & Brothers, 1954.

Williams, Don. *The Apostle Paul and Women in the Church*. Ventura, CA: Regal Books, 1982.

Wilson, Paul Scott. *A Concise History of Preaching*. Nashville, TN: Abingdon Press, 1992.

Zahn, T. *Introduction to the New Testament*. Vol. 1. Trans. J. M. Trout. Grand Rapids, MI: Kregel Publications, 1953.

Commentaries

Barclay, William. *The Acts of the Apostles*. Edinburgh, England: The Saint Andrew Press, 1952.

Bruce, F. F. *The Acts of the Apostles: Greek Text with Introduction and Commentary*. Grand Rapids, MI: William B. Eerdmans Publishing Company, 1990.

____. *The Book of the Acts*. Grand Rapid, MI: Wm. B. Eerdmans Publishing Company, 1984.

____. *The Book of the Acts*. rev. ed. Grand Rapids, MI: WM. B. Eerdmans Publishing Co., 1988.

Carter, Charles W. and Ralph Earle. *The Acts of the Apostles*. Grand Rapids, MI:

Zondervan Publishing House, 1978.

Dunn, James D. G. *Romans 9-16: Word Biblical Commentary.* Vol. 38$_B$, Dallas, TX: Word Books Publisher, 1988.

Fung, Ronald Y. K. *The Epistle to the Galatians: The New International Commentary on the New Testament.* Grand Rapids, MI: William B. Eerdmans Publishing Company, 1989.

Hendrikson, William. *I & II Thessalonians.* London: The Banner of Truth Trust, 1972.

Henry, Matthew. *Commentary on the Whole Bible.* Vol. 6. *Acts to Revelation.* Old Tappan, NJ: Fleming H. Revell Company, n.d.

Keener, Craig S. *The IVP Bible Background Commentary: New Testament.* Downers Grove, IL: InterVarsity Press, 1993.

LaSor, William Sanford. *Church Alive: A Bible Commentary for Laymen: Acts.* Glendale, CA: Regal Books, 1952.

Lee, Sang-Keun. *The Acts of the Apostles.* Seoul: The Department of Education of the General Assembly of the Korean Presbyterian Church, 1983.

Lenski R.C.H. *The Interpretation of the Acts of the Apostles II.* Translated by Yeong Bae Cha. Seoul: Baek Hap Publishing Company, 1979.

Maddox, Robert L, Jr. *Layman's Bible Book Commentary: Acts, Vol. 19.* Nashville, Tennessee: Broadman Press, 1979.

Marshall, I. Howard. *The Acts of the Apostles: An Introduction and Commentary.* Grand Rapids, MI: Wm. B. Eerdmans Publishing Company, 1980.

_____. *The Acts of the Apostles: The Tyndale New Testament Commentaries.* Leicester, England: Inter-Varsity Press, 1983.

Park, Yune-Sun. *A Commentary on the Book of the Acts.* Seoul: Yung Eum Sa, 1981.

Phillips, John. *Exploring Acts: Volume Two, Acts 13-28.* Chicago, IL: Moody Press, 1986.

Articles / Periodicals

Allen, Wayne. "When the Mission Pays the Pastor." *Evangelical Missions Quarterly* 34 (April 1998): 176-81.

Barclay, John M. G. "Paul Among Diaspora Jews: Anomaly or Apostate?" *Journal for the Study of the New Testament* 60 (December 1995): 89-120.

Bessenecker, Scott. "Paul's Short-term Church Planting: Can It Happen Again?" *Evangelical Missions Quarterly* 33 (October 1997): 326-32.

Birkey, Del. "The House Church: A Missiological Model." *Missiology* 19 (January 1991): 69-80.

Blevins, J. L. "Acts 13-19: The Tale of Three Cities." *Review and Expositor* 87 (March 1990): 439-50.

Blue, Bradley. "Acts and the House Church." In *The Book of Acts in Its First Century Setting*," ed. David W. J. Gill and Conrad Gempf. 119-222. Grand Rapids, MI: William B. Eerdmans publishing Company, 1994.

Borthwick, Paul. "Short-term Youth Team: Are They Worth It?" *Evangelical Missions Quarterly* 32 (October 1996): 402-3

Brewster, E. Thomas and Elizabeth S Brewster. "What It Takes to Learn a Language and Get Involved with People." *Evangelical Missions Quarterly* 14 (April 1978): 101-5.

Clark, M. "St. Paul the Preacher." *Homiletic and Pastoral Review* 92 (March, 1991): 31-32, 51.

Clarke, A. D. "'Be Imitators of Me': Paul's Model of Leadership." *Tyndale Bulletin* 49 (February 1998): 329-60.

Coggins, Wade. "The Risks of Sending Our Dollar Only." *Evangeilical Missions Quarterly* 24 (July 1988): 204-6.

Conn, Harvie M. "The Money Barrier Between Sending and Receiving Churches." *Evangelical Missions Quarterly* 14 (October 1978): 231-39.

Croy, N. C. "Hellenistic Philosophies and the Preaching of the Resurrection (Acts 17:18,32)." *Novum Testamentum* 39 (January 1997): 21-39.

Dayton, Edward R., and David A. Fraser. "Strategy." In *Perspectives on the World*

Christian Movement, ed. Ralph D. Winter and Steven C. Hawthorne, 569-72. Pasadena, CA: William Carey Library, 1981.

Doughty, D. J. "Luke's Story of Paul in Corinth: Fictional History in Acts 18." *Journal of Higher Criticism* 4 (January 1997): 3-54.

Edanad, A. "The Spirit and the Christian Community according to Acts of the Apostles." *Jeevadhara* 28 (1998) 98-108.

Eisenbaum, Pamela. "Is Paul the Father of Misogyny and Antisemitism?" *Cross Current* 50 (Winter 2000-2001): 506-24.

Ericson, Norman R. "Implications from the New Testament for Testament Contextualization." In *Thoelogy and Mission*, ed. David J. Hesselgrave, 71-85. Grand Rapids, MI: Baker Book House, 1978.

Golz, Lud. "If Paul Got Organized to Reach His Objectives, So Can You." *Evangelical Missions Quarterly* 27 (July 1991): 268-72.

Guillemette, N. "Saint Paul and Women." *East Asia Pastoral Review* 26 (February 1989): 121-33.

Gundry-Volf, Judith M. "Paul on Women and Gender: A comparison with Early Jewish Views." In *The Road from Damascus: The Impact of Paul's Conversion on His Life, Thought, and Ministry*, ed. Richard N. Longenecker, 184-212. Grand Rapids, MI: William B. Eerdmans Publishing Company, 1997.

Harrington, D. J. "Paul and Judaism: 5 Puzzles." *Bible Review* 9 (February 1993): 18-25, 52.

Howell, Don N, Jr. "Mission in Paul's Epistles: Genesis, Pattern, and Dynamics." In *Mission in the New Testament: An Evangelical Approach*, ed. William J. Larkin Jr. and Joel F. Williams, 63-91. Maryknoll, NY: Orbis Books, 1998.

Johne, H. R. "The Prohibitions in the Jerusalem Council's Letter to Gentile Believers." *Wisconsin Lutheran Quarterly* 94 (January 1997): 47-48.

Kaak, Paul. "Provenness." *Evangelical Missions Quarterly* 34 (April 1998): 164-68.

Kornfield, William J. "What Hath Our Western Money and Our Western Gospel Wrought?" *Evangelical Missions Quarterly* 27 (July 1991): 230-36.

Leary, T. J. "The 'Aprons' of St. Paul-Acts 19:12." *Journal of Theological Studies* 41 (February 1990): 527-29.

Lee, Hyung-Ki. "Historical Origin of Evangelical Theology and Evangelical Reformed

Theology in Korea. " In *Bible and Theology vol. 1,* ed. Korean Evangelical Theological Society, 183-98. Seoul: Jung Eum Publishing Co., 1983.

MacArthur, John F., Jr. "The Mandate of Biblical Inerrancy: Expository Preaching." *The Master's Seminary Journal* 1 (Spring 1990): 3-17.

MacIntyre, Donald. "Wired for Life." *Time*, 11 December 2000, 18-23.

Mayhue, Richard L. "Rediscovering Expository Preaching." In *Rediscovering Expository Preaching: Balancing the Science and Art of Biblical Exposition*, ed. Richard L. Mayhue, 3-21. Dallas, TX: Word Publishing, 1992.

McKinney, Carol V. "Which Language: Trade or Minority? " *Missiology* 18 (July 1990): 279-89.

Moon, Sang-Cheol. "Current Status Quo of Korean Missionaires." *The Post Horse* 4 (1994): 1-8.

Motz, Arnell. "What Generation Xers Think about Mission Teams." *Evangelical Missions Quarterly* 32 (October 1996): 409.

Newbigin, Lesslie. "Cross-currents in Ecumenical and Evangelical Understandings of Mission," *International Bulletin of Missionary Research* 6 (October 1982): 146-51.

Nicholls, Kathleen D. "Tell the Story Powerfully in Local Cultural Forms." *Evangelical Missions Quarterly* 19 (October 1983): 298-306.

Norrish, Howard. "Lone Ranger: Yes or No?" *Evangelical Missions Quarterly* 26 (January 1990): 6-12.

Ollog, W. H. "Paulus und seine Mitarbeiter." Neukirchen-Vluyn: Neukirchener Verlag, 1979, 92-122. Quoted in Davide J. Bosch, *Transforming Mission: Paradigm Shifts in Theology of Mission, 132.* Maryknoll, NY: Orbis Books, 1991.

Paimoen, E. "The Importance of Paul's Missionary Team." *Stulos Theological Journal* 4 (February 1996): 157-73.

Pelt, Leslie. "What's Behind the Wave of Short-termers?" *Evangelical Missions Quarterly* 28 (October, 1992): 384-88.

Pocock, Michael. "Gaining Long-term Mileage from Short-term Programs." *Evangelical Missions Quarterly* 23 (April 1987): 154-60.

Racey, David. "Contextualization: How Far is Too Far?" *Evangelical Missions Quarterly* 32 (July 1996): 304-9.

Rook, J. "Women in Acts: Are They Equal Partner with Men in the Earliest Church?" *McMaster Journal of Theology* 2. (February 1991): 29-41.

Sanchez, Daniel. "Contextualization and the Missionary Endeavor." In *Missiology: An Introduction to the Foundations, History, and Strategies of World Missions*, ed. John Mark Terry, Ebbie Smith and Justice Anderson, 318-33. Nashville, Tennessee: Broadman and Holman Publishers, 1998.

Sandnes, Karl Olav. "Paul and Socrates: The Aim of Paul's Areopagus Speech." *Journal for the Study of the New Testament* 50 (June 1993): 17-20.

Sawatsky, Ben. "What It Takes To Be a Church Planter." *Evangelical Missions Quarterly* 27 (Oct. 1991): 342-47.

Sciberras, P. "The Figure of Paul in the Acts of the Apostles: The Areopagus Speech." *Melita Theologica* 43 (January 1992): 1-15.

Shaw, R. Daniel."Cultural and Evangelism: A Model for Missiological Strategy." *Missiology* 18 (July 1990): 291-304.

Shillington, G. "Paul's Success in the Conversion of Gentiles: Dynamic Center in Cultural Diversity." *Directuon* 20 (February 1991): 125-34.

Sklba, R. "Paul of Tarsus: A Model for Diocesan Priesthood." *Emmanuel* 104 (August 1998): 453-64.

Stott, John R. W. "The Living God Is A Missionary God." In *Perspectives on the World Christian Movement*, ed. Ralph D. Winter and Steven C. Hawthorne, A-18. Pasadena, CA: William Carey Library, 1992.

Suggit, J. N. "'The Holy Spirit and We resolved ...'(Acts 15:28)." *Journal of Theology for Southern Africa* 79 (1992): 38-48.

Unpublished Materials / Interviews

Alfredo, Carlos. Telephone interview by researcher, March 12, 2001

Casiño, Tereso C. "Preaching Workshop in Bible Exposition." Lecture given at the Visayas Nazareth Bible College chapel in Cebu City, Philippines on February 6,

2001. Library of Cebu Bible College, Cebu City, Philippines.

"Directory of Churches and Pastors of Visayas Presbytery". Cebu, Philippines: Visayas Presbytery, 1999.

"Directory of Churches. Souvenir Program," 5th General Assembly of the Presbyterian Church of the Philippines, Dasmarinas City, Cavite, October 17-18, 2000.

Hur, Jin-Phil. Telephone interview by researcher, March 1, 2001.

Hwang, Sung-Gon. Telephone interview by researcher, March 1, 2001.

Jee, Young-Ku. Telephone interview by researcher, March 8, 2001.

Jung, Jooo-Chae. "Life of Thanksgiving." Sermon preached at the Jamsil Central Church in Seoul on November 21, 1999. Cebu Bible College Library, Mandaue City, Philippines.

Kim, Byung-Yoon. "An Analysis of the Church Planting Methods of Korean Evangelical Missionaries in the Philippines." Th.D. diss., Asia Baptist Graduate Theological Seminary, 1998.

Kim, Hwal-Young. "From Asia to Asia: A History of Cross-Cultural Missionary Work of the Presbyterian Church in Korea (Hapdong), 1959-1992." D.Miss. diss., Reformed Theological Seminary, 1993.

Kim, Jae-Sung. Personal interview by researcher, January 9, 2001, Cebu City.

Kim, Young-Mi. Telephone interview by researcher, March 8, 2001.

Kim, Yong-Woo. Personal letter to researcher on March 9, 2001.

Kwon, Soon-Tae. "An Analysis of the Contemporary Models of Missions Among the Selected Baptist Churches in Seoul, Korea in the Light of Paul's Model of Missions." Th.D. diss., Asia Baptist Graduate Theological Seminary, 2000.

Matulac, Edmund. "Annual Statistical Report" Souvenir Program, the 9th Stated Meeting of the Visayas Presbytery, Davao City, December 5-6, 2000.

Moon, Steve S. C. "The Acts of Koreans: A Research Report on Korean Missionary Movement." http://www.krim.org.files/ The_Acts_of_Koreans.doc. Internet; Accessed 3 December 2001.

Presbyterian Church of the Philippines, "PILIPINAS." n.p., 1990.

Rho, Jeong-Hee. Telephone interview by researcher, February 26, 2001.

The Office of the General Secretary of the General Presbytery of the Presbyterian Church of the Philippines. "The Minutes of the General Presbytery of the Presbyterian Church of the Philippines (From Inaugural Session to 19th Assembly: June 27, 1987 – October 5,6, 1994)." Quezon City, Philippines: n.p.,1995.

Visayas Presbytery, "The 8th Stated Meeting of the Visayas Presbytery," June 6-7, 2000, Cebu Shalom Presbyterian Church.

PHOTOS

Photo 1: Missionary Dispatching Service for Rev. Dr. Hoo-Soo Jose Nam on August 26, 1987 in Ulsan Presbyterian Church (a member of the Korean Presbyterian Church (Ko-Shin) denomination) in South Korea.

Photo 2: Rev. and Mrs. Hoo-Soo Jose Nam and Rev. and Mrs. Hyung-Kyu Kim take oath during the Missionary dispatching service in South Korea.

Photo 3: KPCK Missionary families.

The second line from left - Rev. & Mrs. Sung-Il Kim, Rev. & Mrs. Sung-Ju Shin, Mrs. Choi, Mrs. and Rev. Kyung-Keun Lee, Rev. Kwang-Suk Choi.

The first line from left - Mrs. Nam, children of Rev. and Mrs. Hoo-Soo Jose Nam, Rev. & Mrs. Jae-Yong Kim, and Rev. Hoo-Soo Jose Nam.

Photo 4: The Iligan Presbyterian Church building in Mindano Province in the Philippines.

Photo 5: Rev. Hoo-Soo Jose Nam baptizing a church member of Iligan Presbyterian Church in the Philippines.

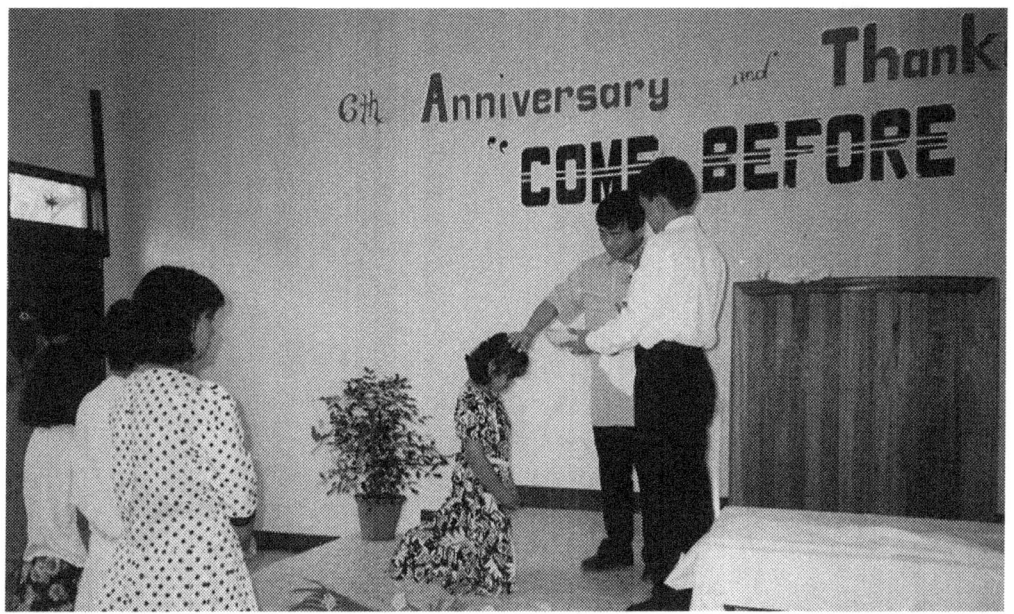

Photo 6: Rev. Dr. Hoo-Soo Jose Nam gives a special lecture on Christian Missions at a local Filipino church.

Photo 7: Sunday worship service at Baybay Presbyterian Church, a Filipino church planted by Rev. Dr. Hoo-Soo Jose Nam. The worship leader is Rev. Nicolas Loreto, Filipino clergyman.

Photo 8: Surigao Presbyterian Church members and their bamboo church building.

Photo 9: Rev. Dr. Hoo-Soo Jose Nam hosts the families of his Christian clergy co-workers during the pastors' family retreat in a beach resort in the Philippines.

Photo 10: The first officers of Visayas Presbytery.

From the left – Rev. Efren Azarcon (clerk), Rev. Yong-Woo Kim (vice moderator), Rev. Dr. Hoo-Soo Jose Nam (moderator), Rev. Edmund Matulac (general secretary), Rev. Kwang-Suk Choi (treasurer).

Photo 11: In October, 1998, Rev. Hoo-Soo Jose Nam (left), the Moderator of the General Assembly of the Presbyterian Church of the Philippines (GA – PCP), announces to the General Assembly that Rev. Sung-Ho Nahm (second from the left) is the new Moderator.

Photo 12: As a part of the missions program of the Korean Presbyterian Church (Ko-Shin) denomination, Rev. Dr. Hoo-Soo Jose Nam opened the Presbyterian Vocational Institute of the Philippines where trainees learn sowing and the Word of Christ in preparation for making a living as well as for becoming Christian witnesses.

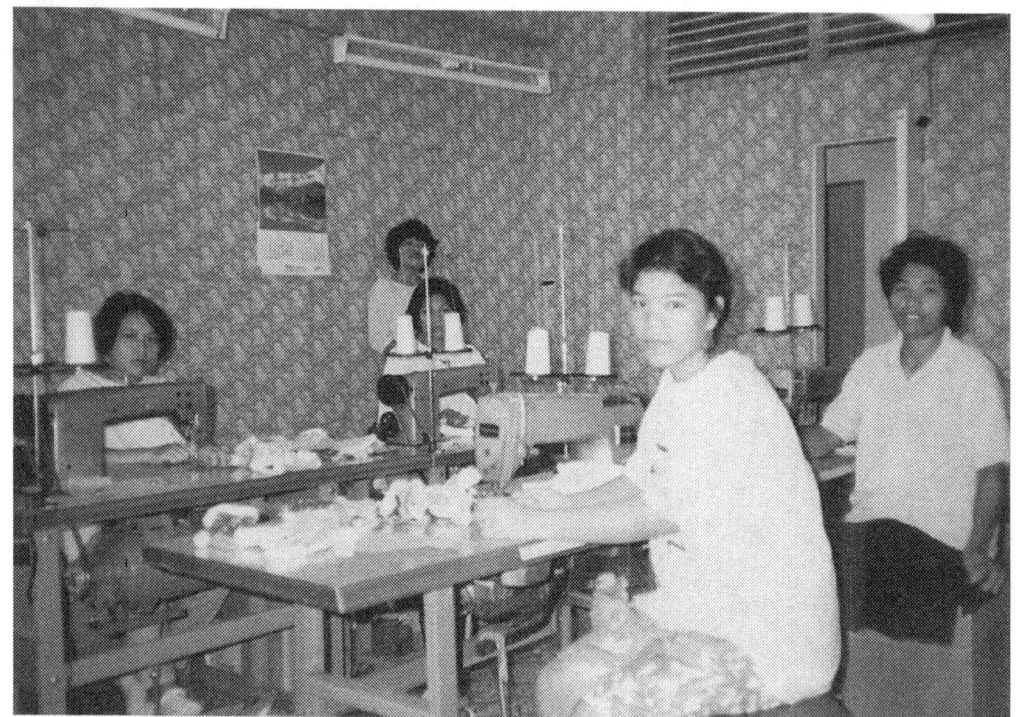

Photo 13: Rev. Hoo-Soo Jose Nam receives the degree of Doctor of Theology (Th.D.) from Asia Baptist Graduate Theological Seminary in Baguio, Philippines.

From right – Rev. Dr. Kwang-Soo Lee (a Korean Baptist Missionary), Mrs. Nam, Mrs. Lee, Rev. Dr. Hoo-Soo Jose Nam.

Photo 14: The first commencement exercise of Cebu Bible College.

First line from left – Rev. Efren Azarcon (Dean of Student), Dr. Se-Hyun Kim (Academic Dean), Dr. Hoo-Soo Jose Nam (President), Dr. Hee-Koo Yoon (Chairman of the Board), Mrs. Euly Matulac (Registrar).

Second line from left – Rev. Edmund Matulac (Dorm Supervisor), Mr. Tarex Pongcol (graduate), Miss Elena Leocadio (graduate), Mr. Willie Dindin (graduate), Mrs. Sung-Hee Nam (Business Manager).

Photo 15: Rev. Hoo-Soo Jose Nam preaches at a local Filipino church.

Photo 16: Cebu Bible College students are learning to be Christian leaders in the Philippines.

Photo 17: Rev. Hoo-Soo Jose Nam and Rev. Edmund Matulac officiate at the wedding of an international couple; the bride is a Filipino and the groom is a Korean.

ABSTRACT

The title of this dissertation is, "An Analysis of the Missions Strategies of the Korean Presbyterian Missionaries in Central and Southern Philippines in the Light of Paul's Missions Strategies." The statement of the problem is as follows: "What are the missions strategies of the Korean Presbyterian missionaries in central and southern Philippines from 1990 to 2000, which can be analyzed in the light of Paul's missions strategies? " In response to this problem, three sub-problems were examined with the use of literary research and field survey.

Chapter One dealt with the following first sub-problem: "What are Paul's missions strategies evident in Acts 13-28?" Prior to conducting this study the researcher assumed that "Paul employed missions strategies that could be ascertained in Acts 13-28." In dealing with this problem the researcher chose Paul's six missions strategies as endorsed by scholars and their relevance to the Korean Presbyterian missionaries in central and southern Philippines. These strategies are as follows: (1) strategies in planting church, (2) strategies in preaching the gospel, (3) strategies in equipping leaders, (4) strategies in financing ministries, (5) strategies in team ministries, and (6) strategies in contextualized communication.

The first chapter investigated Paul's missions strategies in Acts 13-28 as the fundamental principles for all missions work down through history. If missionaries were aware of these biblical principles of missions strategies prior to arrival on the fields, they could reduce mistakes and have a more effective ministry. When Paul planted churches, he always tried to choose a strategic location, selected receptive people, and employed effective methods. Paul understood the socio-political situations and the anthropo-geography of the Roman Empire. The study showed how Paul could discern a strategic location, find receptive people, and utilize creative methods in church planting ministries.

The study noted that Paul had a clear understanding of his tasks, which he received from God. This determined the content of his message, with Jesus Christ as central. The starting point of Paul's preaching varied according to his audience and circumstances, but the conclusion was always Jesus Christ. Basically Paul took a strong stance on non-Christian religions and did not compromise with them. He creatively approached the people of other religions with care. The characters of Paul's message were discussed as well.

The study pointed out the importance of local leadership in the church. To install local leadership of the church, Paul chose locally proven people following the initiative and guidance of the Holy Spirit. Paul creatively mobilized women leadership in his missions work. He would train local leaders with the following three foundations: doctrinal foundation, practical foundation, and spiritual foundation. The methods Paul utilized for local leadership training program were also examined. Paul needed financesfor managing missions teams. His ministries, however, did not depend on financialsupport. He had two financial strategies, namely, self-supporting missionary and self-supporting church.

Paul worked with his missions team, stressing on team ministry as one of his prominent strategies. A profile of his team ministry was examined in this chapter. As the leader of his missions team, how Paul managed his team members to work effectivelywas explored.

Paul was a Hellenistic Jew and was educated in Jerusalem, but his ministry extended beyond the geographical and cultural boundaries of Judaism. He crossed boundaries successfully, and understood people's cultural differences. Paul knew how to connect multi-cultures for the sake of the gospel. As a multi-cultural missionary, Paul invested a significant effort to make his message relevant to local contexts. The study revealed how well Paul contextualized his message in each culture such as Judaism and Hellenism. The study also showed how attentively Paul employed a well-contextualized methods each time he encountered different cultures in different places. Paul knew how to shift the paradigm of his message promptly whenever he confronted people from other regions like monotheists, polytheists, and pantheists.

Chapter Two dealt with the following second sub-problem: "What are the missions strategies of the Korean Presbyterian missionaries in central and southern Philippines from 1990 to 2000? " Before conducting field survey, the researcher assumed that there were identifiable missions strategies respondents employed in their **missionary tasks**. The survey was done in two parts. The first part presented basic information about the missionaries and their work. This includes a brief history of the missions work of the four missions groups of the Korean Presbyterian Church and an analysis of the general information of the missionaries. The brief history section dealt with the history and work of these four Korean Presbyterian missions groups respectively: Korean Presbyterian Church (Ko-sin; KPCK), Korean Presbyterian Church (Hap-dong; KPCH), Korean Presbyterian Church (Tong-hap; KPCT), and Korean Presbyterian Church (Kai-hyuk; KPCKH). Some senior missionaries' history and work were dealt with more than the new missionaries because they were the founders of each missions group. General information about these missionaries consisted of details on ministerial status, age range of the missionaries, length of time in missions work, analysis of ministries, and an analysis of church growth. This part presented the present status of missions work and the numerical growth of the churches and baptized members, national workers, and the missionaries from 1990 to 2000. The statistics showed that the church grew slowly from 1990 to 1994, and then accelerated from 1995 onwards as missionaries gained more experiences, not to mention the increase of national workers.

The second part showed and analyzed the missions strategies of the Korean Presbyterian missionaries in central and southern Philippines including planting church, preaching the gospel, equipping leaders, financing ministry, team ministry, and contextualized communication. Date from the field survey were presented according to the pattern used in Chapter One for the sake of correlation. This part presented the results of the field survey that analyzed and interpreted the questionnaires using statistical tools.

Chapter Three dealt with the following third sub-problem: "What are the strengths and weaknesses of the Korean Presbyterian missionaries in central and southern

Philippines from 1990 to 2000?" Prior to conducting the study, the researcher assumed that there were strengths and weaknesses in the missions strategies employed by the Korean Presbyterian missionaries in central and southern Philippines, in relation to Paul's missions strategies and to the growth of the church for which these missionaries have worked. The researcher noticed seven strengths and seven weaknesses.

In this chapter the researcher noted that most Korean Presbyterian missionaries in central and southern Philippines demonstrated a high level of evangelistic fervor. This affirmed Paul's emphasis on sharing the gospel and fulfilling the Great Commission. Spiritual sensitivity was one of the perceived strengths of the missionary respondents. The spiritual aspect was one of the highest concerns for the missionaries. Holding astrong identity as a Presbyterian and retaining a Calvinistic reformed theology was another identifiable strength. The fact that Korean ministers dislike changing their denominational affiliation contributed to church growth in central and southern Philippines. Most of these missionaries wanted to cooperate with national church leaders. This desire for cooperation led them to begin equipping local ministers. The respondents' persistence to equip national leaders was one noticeable strength. At the same time, they showed willingness to transfer leadership tasks to local leaders. Another area of strength noted was the parental responsibility of the missionaries for the newly planted churches. These missionaries did not abandon churches they planted, but they committed the church to the Holy Spirit and tried to care for them, even after turning over the leadership to local leaders. The fact that these missionaries endeavored to adopt the local culture was the other identifiable strength.

In conducting the literary research and field survey, the researcher discovered the following specific areas of weakness in the missions strategies of these missionaries. The first noticeable weakness was the language problem. This was one of the greatest weaknesses because most of the other weaknesses were derived from their poor ability to speak English and the local language. Another area of identifiable weakness was found in their lack of enthusiasm to contextualize the practice of local ministries . Most missionary-respondents seemed to have the opinion that the practice of ministry in Korean church is universally applicable. This resulted in the stereotyping of ministry in the Philippines, which does not fit Filipino church setting. There was an evident lack of understanding the Filipino cultural value systems on the part of missionary-respondents. The research also showed the tendency to mishandle finances in the mission field. Most missionary-respondents have a tendency to control missions funds without sharing fund management with their Filipino counterparts. Another weakness noted was the sometimes unreasonable influence of supporting churches in Korea, although they do not possess a good understanding about the missions fields. In many cases, supporting churches would hold the financial resources, which results in limiting the ability of the missionaries to work effectively and autonomously. Noted also was the lack of information about the trend in world missions and other socio-political aspects that affect missions work. Overall, the study showed inadequate teamwork among missionaries from the same groups, between missionaries and the national coworkers, and between missionaries and the supporting bodies in Korea.

In the light of the above summary of findings of the study, the following implications seem to be appropriate as noted thus:

1. There is a need for Korean missionaries to acknowledge the necessity of overcoming the language barriers and to improve their langue learning skills. Sufficient time and resources must be given to them both in Korea and in the Philippines.

2. Korean missionaries need to be exposed in various aspects of cross-cultural missions settings prior to their deployment. To surmount a narrow-minded worldview caused by mono-language, mono-race, and mono-culture society, a multi-cultural training setting under a qualified mentor, both in Korea and in the Philippines is recommended.

3. In order to understand Filipino people deeper, missionaries need to study the Filipino value systems prior to serving in the missions field. This requires a good deal to anthropological studies of the target people even before encountering them face to face.are required.

4. There is a need to develop alternative plans for the arrangement of missions funds. The current practice of controlling missions funds alone by missionaries need reconsideration. There is a need to formulate a biblically-sound financial principle that would be made clear to supporting churches in Korea, missionaries in the field, and national leaders in the Philippines.

5. There is a need for missionary sending bodies to trust and support the missions strategies which on-the-field missionaries have formulated according to contextual needs and environments.

6. Sufficient information of modern missions trend and other socio-political information both international and local are compulsory for missionaries. Thus, supporting churches and missions agencies need to supply information by sending newspapers, magazines, journals, and other materials. For prompt supply of information, networking of the professionals in this area should be encouraged.

7. In the light of the Korean Presbyterian missionaries' pattern of working independently, team spirit should be encouraged. The practice of duplicating missions investment in the same areas need to be avoided at all costs. This calls for a creation of a council among missionaries and missions agencies from different denomination to serve as a networking agency to avoid waste of missions resources.

8. To meet the increasing need of highly educated missionaries or professionals, especially in the area of theological education, incoming missionaries need to receive training on the highest level prior to their field assignment. Career missionaries should be encouraged to use their furlough for additional education..

9. Alongside formal theological education in the missions field, missionaries need practical discipleship training in various situations.

10. As majority of the missionary-respondents tend to work in urbanized areas, there is a need to rethink missions strategies, which include giving more attention to tribal or regional people groups, particularly the Muslims in Mindanao and other areas. For this purpose, missionaries need to take advanced training that specialize on how to reach out particular ethno-linguistic people groups in the Philippines.

About the Author

Rev. Dr. Hoo-Soo Jose Nam is the Director of Koshin Missions Training Institute, which is the official missionary training organization of the Korean Presbyterian Church (Ko-Shin) denomination, one of the three biggest Presbyterian denominations in South Korea. Rev. Dr. Nam was the Visiting Professor of Korea Theological Seminary in South Korea from 2003 to 2004.

Rev. Dr. Hoo-Soo Jose Nam has been a historic figure in the Presbyterian movement in the Philippines. He planted 10 Filipino Presbyterian churches, and was instrumental in the founding of the Presbyterian Church of the Philippines, one of the biggest Presbyterian denomination in the Philippines. He served as the moderator of the Visayas Presbytery in 1995. And he was the Moderator of the General Assembly of the Presbyterian Church of the Philippines in 1996.

Rev. Dr. Hoo-Soo Jose Nam was the President of Cebu Bible College from 1995 to 2003 and trained many Presbyterian clergy and Presbyterian leaders for the Philippines during that time.

Rev. Dr. Hoo-Soo Jose Nam is ordained in the Korean Presbyterian Church (Ko-Shin) and holds the M.Div. degree from Korea Theological Seminary and a Th.D. from Asia Baptist Theological Graduate Seminary.

Rev. Dr. Hoo-Soo Jose Nam is married to Sung-Hee Eunice (Lee) Nam and has two children. His son is Hwa-Peong Timothy Nam and currently serving in the Korean military, and his daughter is Hae-Sun Keren Nam is a student at Korea University, majoring in international politics.